BEYOND THE TAILGATE

How Tailgating Brings and Keeps Friends and Families Together

Jim and Cheryl Flint '94

DEDICATION

"Clear eyes, full hearts, can't lose."
—Coach Eric Taylor, *Friday Night Lights*

TABLE OF CONTENTS

ACKNOWLEDGMENTS

I want to start by thanking my incredible best friend and wife of more than twenty-five years, Cheryl. From her willingness to participate in the original tailgating journey to revisiting our experiences for this book, she keeps making my dreams come true. I pinch myself to see when or if I'll ever wake up. My friends say it so often, and it's so true—I out kicked my coverage. Thank you for sharing your life with me.

To the football family men in our lives. To Foster Flint, our beloved Dad, who's taught the next generation of his family how to love sports and share experiences. Your unique passion for sports, love of numbers and creativity sensibilities helps keep us grounded--yet excited--about the possibilities of what's ahead.

To Andrew Christian, Flint Christian, and Philip Christian—you are loved for who you are and for sharing in each other's lives—fantasy football, family, tailgates, or otherwise.

Thanks to Cindy Christian for being a great sister and showing the world and our family how courageous one can be in dealing with cancer.

To Joshua, Amy and Whitman Wolfshohl, we love you for being one of the best parts of our family. We love to spend time with you at football games, at the beach house, or places all over the world.

To my Mom for being a creative force throughout my childhood. Her insights influence me to this day. Thank you for being so supportive of athletics throughout my childhood, so much so that you couldn't help but fall in love with sports.

Thanks to everyone on the Varsity Tailgaters team with particular emphasis to David, Sarah, Amy, Albert and Whitney, who helped build the tailgate. Additional kudos to Josh, Marty, Lauren, Chris, Cameron, Lindsay, and Teddy for all the setups and breakdowns. Special thanks to John Burr and John Montgomery, who took our tailgate to the next level.

Thanks to the entire Trahan family, but especially to Vince, Becky, Jeff, Jenny, and Austin.

Thanks to Ellen and Joel Yelton. Trahans, you brought the family. Yeltons, you are great friends who feel like family. Each of you helped us keep the core of our tailgate about family and friends.

Much appreciation to Jill Welsh, who now holds the distinction of having successfully edited three of my books.

An additional acknowledgment goes out to David Lamm, founder of Tailgating Ideas, for bringing tailgaters around the country together via his website TailgatingIdeas.com and for encouraging me to repurpose the many "Tailgating Ideas" I've written throughout the years in the pages of this book.

PROLOGUE

The experiences we share in the pages that follow have taught us how to approach our lives and relationships. Please, join us. We'd like to share some great stories with you. If you will, let's start with one of the most famous stories of all time.

Do you remember Jack from the childhood fairy tales your parents told you?

No, not the Jack from *Jack and Jill* fame, who went up the hill to fetch a pail of water. No, not even our very own "Jack and Jill," the namesakes of our two SPCA kitties that routinely charm us with their rare combination of mischievousness, innocence, and aplomb. Indeed, our Jack and Jill bring us so much joy.

No, we speak of "Jack," the guy with the magic beans who woke the sleeping giant. We want to be your Jack and wake the sleeping giants in you as we share our experiences of how Texas A&M's move to the Southeastern Conference (SEC) and our participation in tailgates "woke" so many of us.

Beyond the Tailgate captures Texas A&M's once-in-a-lifetime journey into the SEC while our family and friends helped us build a bigger, bolder, bonding tailgate experience. In the pages that follow we also go "Beyond the Tailgate" to share how a football foundation further cemented our friendship and relationship.

During the moments that mattered, we may not have known how or even why the connections and experiences we had would matter so much, but we now know that they did.

And as you read through the pages, know that while football is core to the conversation, the real stadium lights, if you will, that keep the game in its proper perspective, include the playing field of relationships.

Each chapter tells a story from two points of view: "Our View" and "Cheryl's Thoughts." Jim's the writer, but Cheryl's insights and experiences cut to the chase of what brings so many couples to the games. Her voice comes from a view of how sports serve as a love language in our families.

The fears and motivations we each had were different, but the experiences and shared history we developed brought us, as well as those around us, closer together.

Think of Jack as you read the pages that follow and stay woke to your sleeping giants and all the possibilities that exist beyond the tailgate.

Gig 'Em Aggies!

INTRODUCTION

The experiences we share in the pages that follow have taught us how to approach our lives and relationships.

Tailgating reminded Cheryl how much she enjoyed people and how important social engagements are. I work a lot. And it's good to have a channel that keeps you focused on how important your family and friends are.

The teamwork involved in tailgating involves our core partnership and communication via the love language of sports. Cheryl loves watching how happy people are and how much energy they bring to the table in the realm of sports. As she notes: "It's fascinating." Sports—and tailgates by extension— have a tendency to make things bigger. The bonding experiences we share become amplified and long-lasting.

We —in this process of writing the book—relearned why we fell in love with each other. In the beginning, middle and end there was a great deal of thinking about others before thinking about ourselves.

Additionally some timely decisions along the way helped ensure that we took care of ourselves as we took care of our others.

The purpose of sharing these words and experiences is to remember the life and experiences that occurred at the tailgate. As time marches on, we realize there's so much more about life, tailgating, and each other that allows us to continue growing. The more we learn, the less we know.

We'd like to share with you the growth experiences and stories that evolved over a decade or more of tailgating. May it help you and yours make any, if not every, important event even bigger, brighter, bolder, and better.

The common threads of time, love, energy, people, and our positive shared histories connect us as humans. There's a ton to the tailgate, but there's so much more beyond the tailgate, too. We hope you share in our love of sports, family, friends, and food. Enjoy!

Chapter 1

※

Humble and Hungry

"Don't worry about the pressure or the responsibility. Just live in it, have fun, and when everything seems to be going right, just stay humble and remember your family."

—*Roman Reigns, American professional wrestler*

Our View

Our first tailgates started humbly.

At some level, so too did our relationship. High school sweethearts, we went to different colleges and attended games together even before we married. Looking back on over twenty-five years provides some perspective. Here are some notes from our first game together at Texas A&M.

<u>11-13-1993 vs. Louisville – 42 to 7 – Win</u>

One of the first Texas A&M games my wife and I attended together was in 1993. We were engaged at the time and had the opportunity to pet Reveille VI, A&M's collie mascot, as a puppy during the game in which he took over for the retiring Reveille V.

Pregame tailgating didn't exist back then—especially like it does today, but there was a feeling that we'd be back.[1]

We were engaged on January 1, 1993, and married on Saturday, January 1, 1994, in the late afternoon. During the reception, Texas A&M played Notre Dame in the Cotton Bowl. Given that Cheryl's grandfather, P.E. Skloss, was one of five brothers and two sisters, there were plenty of Aggies and other sports fans at the wedding. Her uncles, my family, and even Father Tony—a Notre Dame fan—were pleased to know that the game would be on a television at the reception that day. Today, the ubiquity of smartphones would make this item less of an issue, but Cheryl's receptiveness to having a game on television at our wedding reception set the stage for things to come. Sports, it seems, would help to bring and keep the people in our life together.

Twenty-five years of marriage later we still attend events and spend time with family and friends at tailgates. Somewhere in the middle of that time, we ran a tailgate for an amazing twelve years. In the pages that follow, we share many of those experiences with the idea that there's so much to the tailgate, but so much more *beyond* the tailgate. As you move beyond the tailgate, you will notice that relationships and conversations and associations with your family and friends will occur more naturally. May your passion for sports and football be equally matched by the passion you have for your relationships.

As driving forces go, our first tailgates came from a passion for the sport and, at some level, a desire to spend more time with family and friends. The alternative involved sitting in traffic.

At the time, the Aggies' Kyle Field held over 82,000 people. The traffic patterns before and after games meant you would spend an additional 90 minutes both before and after just waiting for traffic to clear. Add another 90 minutes for the actual trip each way, and you were in the car as much as you were at the game. The offshoot of all that time in traffic, ultimately, developed into plans to arrive four hours before and stay four hours after the games. That, plus the four-hour game itself, resulted in a full, yet much more fulfilling, 12-hour day of tailgating.

Our initial tailgating solution grew into so much more. Initially a small handheld cooler and folding lawn chairs gave us refuge from the traffic. Our families and friends gave us the energy and the fuel that we needed to grow. We found an inauspicious location on the backside of the Reed Arena basketball stadium parking lot to start our football tailgating.

At the time, I (Jim) saw the potential of what it could be. Texas A&M was—and arguably still is—a sleeping giant in the world of collegiate athletics. With loyal fans, huge operating budgets, and some of the best facilities in the nation, it would make sense for the Aggies to go to the next level. The initial thinking was that the Aggies would be able to compete for a national title after they moved from the Southwest Conference into the Big XII. Talk about a sleeping giant.

As I once said to one of our key tailgate contributors, "Do you know how big this could be?"

We live in the northwest Houston suburb of Cypress, which just happens to be 71 miles from Kyle Field. As we moved through the years, our tailgating goal was simply for it to get a little bit better each year. We would have failed and been more stressed out if we had gone too far or too fast. The lens of one year worked for us. Each year improved our tailgating location and ultimately reached an absolutely prime location. Each year we improved our game-day operations. Each year we added more of the right people to the team. Each year we dealt with the problems. There wasn't a secret moment in time when it all came together, just a myriad of moments that kept us going and growing.

We dealt with sporadic growth, in part by embracing a schedule that ironically required absolute flexibility.

Other than the first three weeks of the season, most of the football games had six-day or thirteen-day TV windows. This meant that the timing of the game would not be known until possibly six days before the game was played. Whether a game started at 11:00 am, 2:30 pm, or 6:00 pm changed everything for the tailgate and, at some level, the attendance, as well as the overall attitude of participants. Additionally, the level of athletic competition helped determine the level of participation for our family and friends. At either extreme, you'd secure huge crowds and interest for a 2:30 pm game versus a nationally ranked Alabama squad or little interest in a chilly or rainy game at 11:00 a.m. versus a Football Championship Subdivision (FCS) school.

How do you maintain the flexibility and communication with so many moving parts?

Over the years, we learned a few lessons along the way that held true in both our tailgating and personal lives. As we moved from the back recesses of the parking lot into a more visible location, the level of focus increased, and our ability to be flexible actually improved. We leaned into the idea that remaining flexible would ultimately keep us from getting bent out of shape.

One of the most visible aspects of our shared journey involved the five-year trip that led us to ultimately arrive, in the aforementioned prime tailgating location, at the corner of Kimbrough and Olsen. Tens of thousands of people walked by our tailgate each weekend at that location. This high-profile position made it easier for us to be seen and found. Essentially, this progress brought about good things, but as all good things do, it came with consequences. Both good and bad. More on that later.

One of the biggest reminders of the difficulties that can occur during tailgating and your relationships is that many, many others exist just beyond the boundaries of your tailgate. Your neighbors do affect you. No matter where you live or what you do, your neighbors matter. During one of our early years of tailgating—as we were in the aforementioned process of moving from the back of the campus to the front—we ended up bouncing around from week-to-week through the middle of the Reed Arena parking lot. On one memorable weekend, we ended up next to tailgating neighbors who had the core tailgating philosophy of "stuff gets messed up at tailgates." Beyond our tailgate, our neighbors ran hard, partied harded and were destructive.

Our sentiment is that most people are good-hearted and

mean well. Most tailgaters have a love of the game and love being around people. The cumulative positive shared experiences over time are remarkable; however, that particular crew—which isn't representative of most experiences we've had —had a different mind-set.

Some tailgaters define themselves by whether or not their team wins or loses. Ours was more about having a positive attitude and developing a positive shared history. There will be great years; there will be bad years. A tailgate and your relationships really have nothing to do with those outcomes. This is an important concept to embrace. In the bigger picture, if you're doing something because you think you will win or you are in a relationship because you think you will be advantaged, you're probably in it for the wrong reasons. Given the cyclical nature of life and sports, you will sooner or later--lose.

Dealing with the Difficulties

One of our key calling cards as tailgaters was our tech savviness. Early on, we were one of the first tailgates to have a radar dish that would allow us to watch the Aggies games as well as the other football games of the day. As it turned out, a few of the people beyond our tailgate had a little too much to drink and began throwing footballs around our radar dish. One direct hit by the football and the radar would be knocked off its trajectory via a spectacular crash that would have undoubtedly damaged the dish, as well as the tethered televisions.

During one tailgate, an adult in our group caught one of the errant throws from one of the athletically minded, if not athletically talented adults, hell bent on testing limits by throwing the football closer and closer to our radar dish. Our friend confronted and returned the football via some frank conversation. Cooler heads prevailed. However, we had to address an uncomfortable situation. That's when one of our infamous tailgating lines came to fruition when our next-door tailgater dismissed the antics of his tailgating team: "Hey, man, things are gonna get *messed* up at a tailgate." Whether our neighbor meant that the people, himself, or expensive equipment were going to be messed up, we knew this was not a long-term neighborhood meant for us. Later, check out Chapter 9 where we reference reputation. Your relationships and friendships extend beyond the tailgate, and hoping for someone to change their ways would not have yielded meaningful results in any foreseeable scenario that we could imagine.

So, we took the higher road and moved to a better location the next week. We would have preferred to make location adjustments like that one at the end of the tailgating year; however, we stayed flexible and made the change the following week to a new and improved location—absent the drama and confrontations required with bad neighbors.

Knowing we were in a bad situation helped us find our next place, which was better. We kept moving to a better destinations. We addressed the issues. Galvanized around them and made a choice to keep moving forward.

As we moved and grew, we added to our real estate and our setup by adding tents. Looking back, it seems akin to adding hotels and motels in Monopoly. When we first started, we had no tent, but by year two, we had our first 10' x 10' tent. After a decade, we had more than eight 10' x 10' tents, as well as additional tents of varying sizes.

A quick checklist of items that we acquired—incrementally through the years—as we simultaneously built positive shared histories and our tailgate:

- Eight pop-up tents;
- Five sponsors;
- Two 60" HD TVs;
- Two Honda A2000 generators;
- Two Winegard satellite antennas;
- Over 35 chairs;
- Five tables for food:
- A Wells Cargo trailer to carry it all;
- A cook team; and
- Memories to last a lifetime.

It may be unreasonable to think you can start tailgating with a list like this, nor would we recommend it. For our relationships that developed, we don't have a list of any kind with regard to the connections that occurred, nor do we plan on trying to develop one. It's a wonderful journey.

Tailgate Crashing Guide

Another sign of our continued growth—both as a couple and as a team of tailgaters—was when we decided to take one weekend off during the year to celebrate and connect with other tailgaters. We went to the game, but we weren't responsible for the activities, the coordination, and the operations. We spent one weekend a year "tailgate crashing".

Just like any football season, every good tailgate needs a bye week, not only to help you recharge your batteries, but also to get a sampling of what goes on at the tailgates around your stadium.

When do you schedule a tailgating bye week? Sometimes the game schedule makes it all too obvious.

Back-to-back games can be too much, and when Texas A&M opens with three consecutive home games. During the middle week, we checked out the other tailgates in and around Kyle Field.

After determining your bye week, the movie *Wedding Crashers* can help to get a game plan together. Here's a list of five things to do to help enhance your tailgate crashing experience.

#5 – Bring your charisma and energy. *Wedding Crashers* as a movie was okay, but Vince Vaughn and Owen Wilson carried the show. You and your team of tailgate crashers must bring your "A game."

#4 – Determine the size of the tailgate-crashing crew. Just two people? Easy. Bring four or more, then you better bring some great stories *or* some food and drink. Or bring cash. More and more, I've noticed big groups that understand the importance of friendly donations.

3 – Determine the goal. This keeps it interesting and gives you a reason to strike up the conversation. I can't tell you how

many people have asked me about our TV and tailgate setup. Reverse the idea and you have the perfect segue into a conversation with anyone at another tailgate. People take pride in what they do well in a tailgating environment, so it's easy to find out about their area of expertise. For example:

What's their favorite tailgating game?

What type of BBQ do they have?

Where did they find that cool inflatable mascot or flag, etc., etc., etc.

#2 – Pick a side. In *Wedding Crashers,* you pick a side of the family to sit with. In tailgate crashing, you pick the color of your team. If it's your home-school tailgate then don't go AWOL on your guys—no matter how poorly they may be performing that year. Primarily, the "pick a side" rule applies to out-of-town tailgate crashing when you don't have a vested interest in who wins the game.

#1 – Don't stay in one place too long. With so many tailgates and so little time keep it moving. You will inevitably meet some very cool people and with the mix of good food, good drink, and great times, it's easy to get caught up in one place. Don't do it though. All season long you're in one place.

On your bye week make sure you keep moving so you can bring the best tailgating ideas back to your future tailgates. To make a smooth transition to your next destination, just invite the people from the spot you're currently at over to your tailgate at the next home game and keep charging ahead.

Look ahead; plan your tailgating bye week when the schedule comes out and you'll be sure to make it a great year.[2]

From our humble beginnings of two lawn chairs and an Igloo cooler we reached our tailgating peak as the Aggie football team reached its peak. One year after being introduced to the SEC and the "Johnny Football" phenomenon, we delivered one of the all-time great tailgates for one of the all-time great games at Kyle Field. An estimated 200,000 people were either in or around Kyle Field that September day in 2013. Just over half of those attendees would be in the stadium and the other half were outside—tailgating—as Alabama avenged a loss from the prior year by the score of 42-35. The game was effectively the collegiate Super Bowl that year.

During that tailgate, I reached over to Cheryl and said, "It doesn't get any bigger than this."

Cheryl's Thoughts

Editor's note: At the end of each chapter Cheryl shares some of her insights into the topics discussed in the chapter.

When I was a student at TAMU, I didn't go to the games. I gave away my tickets for rides to Fort Worth, where my boyfriend, Jimmy Flint, was. Not having much money, you received time and a half to work during the games, so that made more sense for me.

So many years and games later, I've learned to appreciate the college experience as an adult. My dad was a football coach. While I always understood the game, I didn't appreciate them then like I do now. Many people care about winning, but my happiness now comes from being part of a group bigger than myself. I didn't care if they won or not, but enjoyed it more so because of how the winning impacted the people rooting for our team. The energy from the shared experience is awesome. Positive energy is typically better.

Texas A&M has always been an underdog in my view. Maybe less so since we have moved into the SEC, but for the longest time we lived in the shadows of the other schools in the Big 12 or even the Southwest Conference. My history makes it easier to appreciate the victories while not getting down about the defeats. Most fans and our tailgaters stayed connected due to the potential energy. I'm not a competitor, but I am a team player. Those early experiences have also helped me to know that if you get to experience good things later in your life, they will likely be even better and more appreciated. I'm okay with delayed gratification when you're building something bigger than yourself.

My favorite times during the tailgate are at the beginning and the end of the trips. What could be? What will be next week? Potential energy.

During the tailgate it's best to lead with gratitude. I looked forward to connecting each week. With some relationships you only see each other during football season, and I'm grateful to spend time with all the people in an environment we all care about. You connect and bond with people at the tailgate.

Although competition isn't my cup of tea, some of the painful losses are memorable for how they impacted my family and friends. The "one-point-loss year" — we lost back-to-back games to Oklahoma and Nebraska— that November hurt.

However, you keep coming back.[3] We still come back to this day and now we want to give back too. Each tailgate day starts with gratitude for me. When thinking through the experiences, all the issues we have are really first world problems. We have knowledge and experience to adjust to the hard times in life, much less the nuances of a tailgate.

In the end, I really believe my appreciation for the tailgate is from not having experienced it the first time around in college. New experiences teach you to be strong and that there is a brighter future ahead.

I do remember the "Reveille-dog game" vs. Louisville (mentioned to open the chapter), but I was so in tune with the animals and the band that I forgot we were playing a game. It was so cool to hold that puppy. Hold that memory. I hold each tailgate that way in my heart and in my mind to this very day.

Beyond the Tailgate: We enjoyed the growth experiences and accumulated memories. The wins and losses were less important than they otherwise seemed to be in the moment. More than money or time--patience and flexibility meant much more as we all shared our lives and created memories.

CHAPTER 2

Surrounding Forces

Our View

*H*ave you heard the saying that you are the average of the five people you spend the most time with? Jim Rohm, one of America's foremost business philosophers, developed the concept, and we've found it to be true at the tailgate, too. It's also true beyond the tailgate at work and at home.

Whether it's a tailgate, marriage, or life, the early days are typically less complicated. The way our tailgate started, we involved our close friends Amy and Albert because we were going to the games with them during the season. Initially, we only went to one or two games a year and established a mini-tailgate on our own. We prepared food, drinks, and snacks and brought them to the game. Think picnic.

After one of the November games that ended in a close loss—hence all the people in the stadium left the game at the same time—we became stuck in one of the on-campus parking garages. With five levels of parking and only one exit, we spent quite some time talking about the future and what the team and we would do differently next year. With ample time on our hands, we started talking about getting parking passes, which led to the concept of season tickets, which inevitably led to conversations about having larger "picnics."

On Monday morning, Amy, who worked in the same company but in a different department, came into my office and said that she and Albert had decided they wanted to go in with us on season tickets. Suddenly, we were committing to the core of attending six or seven home games a year.

Then another Ag, David, joined the crew, and we had our foundation for positive surrounding forces. Everyone was reliable, accountable and essentially had great attitudes as we signed up and pitched in to attend the games. There wasn't a plan—much less a grand plan—to even have tailgates at this point. We were just excited to be attending games with friends and coworkers and putting together...err...picnics.

As we moved through that first year of tailgating, we found that Cheryl had plenty of family who were either attending classes or, like her, were Former Students. We spent time reconnecting with former classmates, inviting additional coworkers, and making sure that family became a part of our football get togethers. Each Saturday became its own adventure, and it seemed like—especially early on—we were making tremendous strides and huge adjustments each week. Little did we know that was just the beginning.

If we went out and got sunburned the first week, we made sure to bring suntan lotion the next. If the kickoff time moved to 11:00 a.m., we did mimosas and brunch. When the weather forecast predicted rain, we purchased a tent. In the early days, it was wildly unpredictable. We didn't know what we didn't know.

One of the most memorable games happened during our first game as season ticket holders before a 66-8 blowout win versus Southern Methodists University (SMU).

In Texas you hear people from Arizona talk about their "dry heat." On this day it was simply too hot for words. The heat index on the field had to be closer to 150° than to 100°, and there was absolutely no wind. Just sitting in the stadium made me dizzy. I literally saw stars—like in a *Tom and Jerry* cartoon.

At the start of the third quarter there were no less than 2,000 sweat-stained people sitting in the air-conditioned area just outside of the Memorial Stadium Center bookstore in order to beat the heat. The next week, we were sure to bring more water.[4]

And adjust and adjust we did. Again, and again and again. The tailgate teaches you new concepts each week.

As the tailgate evolved we invited friends and families, and looking back we had a lot of contagious energy and excitement in the group. Like attracts like and we were growing quickly.

Naming a Tailgate

In fact, our group became so big that we wanted, if not needed, a tailgate team name. Initially, before we settled into Varsity Tailgaters, we referred to ourselves as the Silver Oak on the

Brazos Tailgaters for two years. Silver Oak is the name of an especially nice wine. The way we figured it; we would celebrate with Silver Oak after wins. However, it ultimately came to mean something entirely different.

If the Aggies won, and since College Station is just off the Brazos River, we'd open up Silver Oak at the postgame tailgate. Great times!

On the drive up for the first game of then Coach Mike Sherman's initial season, one of our newest tailgaters, Sarah, pointed out the window and said, "Hey, we should change our tailgate name. It looks like 'Silver Oak on the Brazos' is the name of a retirement community. That's pretty lame."

Sure enough, whatever self-perceived cool factor we had been working with had been destroyed.

Not so cool of her to mention, but oh so true. The moment turned out to be the equivalent jinx of someone talking about a no-hitter during the middle of a baseball game. Our mojo was under attack and it was only the first game of the season!

Later that evening...somehow...some way...Texas A&M managed to lose to Arkansas State by, in large part, committing four turnovers. When the last of those turnovers occurred with seven seconds left in the game—and right in front of our seats—the silence was powerful. The silent shock wave being sent through the stadium was palpable, and it made my head hurt and ears ring. The silence was deafening. We all knew that it was going to be a long time before things would turn around for the football program much less team.

Our Silver Oak stayed under wraps that night, and we began the process of renaming our tailgating team in earnest.

We became the Varsity Tailgaters after spending a year of doing market research by asking tailgating attendees what they thought the best name should be. We had suggestions from each of our key contributors: friends, family, coworkers, and sponsors.[5]

While we landed on Varsity Tailgaters, we passed on Heisman Tailgaters, Big XII Tailgaters, and Aggie Tailgaters for a number of reasons.

Varsity Tailgaters worked best because, as we did things to build the tailgate, we decided you could either do things at the junior varsity level or the varsity level. We choose to do things at the highest level we reasonably could.

The natural progression in the tailgate world involves inviting family, friends, and like-minded coworkers at first. This involves your sports-minded, competitive people who are interested in the team winning. If this core group isn't "all in," then the tailgating culture and, ultimately, the next-level elements may or may not come together, which holds true beyond the tailgate as well. For those thinking about starting a company or getting married, it's best to be on the same page— and never more so than at the beginning.

Beyond the Tailgate thought: Sure, people say that what happens at the tailgate stays at the tailgate, but with smartphones everywhere, be sure to be on "your own best behavior. An incident at the tailgate reflects poorly on you and those around you. It takes all of five minutes for your tailgate to be filmed and circulated world wide via social media. That can be good...or bad. It's up to you and your fellow tailgaters. See more in Chapter 11 about Social Media Patterns in the SEC.

Family Friendly

You want your tailgate to be family friendly. You just do. However, when you start bringing in parents, aunts, uncles, and cousins, even the little things start to change. Each person has their own set of standards and definitions of appropriateness. Whether your group plays drinking games or plans to be teetotalers, it's in the best interest of attendees to know this before they arrive. Over time we've had various alcohol sponsors and felt compelled to let families know that little ones were welcome—there were hot dogs, Capri Suns, and water for the children—and that we were family friendly in an adult-oriented way. It worked for our attendees.

As first-generation tailgaters, or really first-generation anything, family endorsements can slow things down or speed things up. We've effectively grown up in the era of tailgating, so as the group got bigger and I started writing a blog on TailgatingIdeas.com, they weren't always prepared to understand the growth we were experiencing. First-generation employees of start-up companies can likely relate to this nuanced, somewhat-universal truth.

No matter the case, one of the best things about tailgating is all the wonderful people you will meet. You never know who you might run into.

Coworkers in the Mix

As your tailgate grows, invitations will inevitably go out to
bosses, employees, and clients. It's one thing to invite your peer
group; however, it's an entirely different thing to invite your
boss *or* if you're the boss and decide to invite employees. The
rules adjust a bit and the environment changes subtly, too.
Don't kid yourself. They change because of your relationships
beyond the tailgate. Your boss may be cool. Your employees
may be cool, but tailgating interactions outside of work will
change perceptions. Perception is reality and cuts both ways.
You can improve your image or hurt it. We're just encouraging
you to be aware of the dynamic. This holds true with family,
too, and at some level, with what you do on social media.

Moreover, when you consider the integrated impact of
having your parents, bosses, cousins, employees, and friends all
in the same combustible, excitable environment, you will
quickly learn that you can't even consider, much less control,
all their interactions. As mentioned at the beginning of the
chapter, people, in some ways, help to define themselves by the
people that they hang around. If you believe or accept the
concept that you are the average of the five people you spend
the most time with, then your tailgate and your relationships—
whether you want to acknowledge it or not—are impacted by
the culture. If it's a "free for all" at your home or tailgates,
patience runs short, and craziness ensues. If you have positive
energy, the people at your tailgates will take

the same approach. Again, like attracts like.

Sponsors

Another level of attendance worth mentioning would be sponsors. The concept of and reasoning behind a tailgate recruiting sponsors is completely detailed in Ch. 10 – Getting Sponsored. Sponsors will help you and yours take things to the next level and as such they deserve, if not expect, a little higher level of focus and attention. We wanted to take care of our sponsors because they were taking good care of our tailgaters. In our case, we wanted to share the visibility of a highly marketable location and the positive shared histories we were creating. Additionally, we introduced our sponsors to our community when they came out to a game and thanked them for their support; it helped them connect names and faces with their wonderful products and services.

Our sponsors were big because our location was prominent. We had an occasion when DuPont asked if they could come to our tailgate and use it as part of their recruiting efforts. Apparently, DuPont had talked with one of our collegiate team members—who had advised the recruiter of our high-traffic location—and wanted to use said location to help them recruit interns. At first, I was reluctant, but after understanding that they wanted to use the real estate to prospect for the greater good of higher education, we acquiesced. Not surprisingly, one of our tailgaters landed an internship with and ultimately worked for three years as a process engineer with DuPont through that connection.

Given the cultural elements of bringing so many different forces together, it was important to have guidelines, if not universal truths, to help guide one and all. As we grew, we felt the need to institute a few golden rules for those who wanted to be a part of the Varsity Tailgating program:

Either arrive early to unpack. Or stay late to pack up. Either is appreciated. Both are needed.

Bring food. Bring drinks. Either is appreciated. Both are needed.

If you aren't contributing in either of the aforementioned ways bring positive energy and a good attitude. Both are needed. Either is appreciated.

Failing the above, financial contributions are needed and equally appreciated.

Don't bring your friend's friends without considering all the contributions that are needed to be successful.

If you aren't with us, introduce yourself.

Several years in, we established a wristband system to make sure only select guests were included and that those guests were able to get to know each other. Sure, tailgate crashing is a sport, but it was up to the Varsity Tailgaters in terms of who we brought in and/or kept out.

Family first; friends second.

Be kind to the rival schools. Be friendly because it may be the one impression you make for your own school—win or lose—that makes a difference.

No public displays of affection. Get a room, people.

No Jägermeister (another gracious sponsor) until October.

Rules help with the blending of the groups. The blending of the groups is an amazing experience, but it isn't without growing pains.

On one occasion, one of our most tried-and-true tailgaters brought in a group of four or five coworkers but didn't let anyone know. He also didn't bring any of the aforementioned additional resources. They showed up late, slammed some drinks and food, took a few drinks with them, and didn't show up later to help us break down the tailgate. Over the next week, I reached out to our friend who had, ironically, helped us establish the guidelines. Confronting the behavior is challenging. Our tailgater really thought everything was handled. "There was," he said, "no way all that work was being done by friends and family." Once he learned what it was that he didn't know, he quickly transformed into one of the most generous and conscientious tailgaters we've ever had.

As we think back to the five people who were the biggest part of creating the Varsity Tailgaters, we considered it in terms of the families we spent the most time with at the tailgate. In lieu of listing them individually, it's safe to say they have a good idea of who they are, and we thank them to this day for all their contributions.

As you think about the five people you spend the most time with, we know that the people we work with beyond the tailgate in our daily lives can also take up a big chunk of our time, and there can also be "energy vampires."

This tailgating book isn't a workbook per se, but it's worth taking the time with your spouse to discuss who you are spending the most time with and then decide together if that's who you want to be the average of. It's much easier to see others than it is to see ourselves. We suppose that's why our eyes are facing outward! Take the time to consider who those five people are, and determine if they are the best for you, your family, and your tailgate.

Cheryl's Thoughts

I've really learned so much from the conversations. I'd learn stuff at the tailgate that I could apply to my work week and vice versa. The "people part" of the equation really changed for me from week to week, and now looking back, I can see how different people influenced my experiences. Certainly, sharing positive experiences was fun, but negative experiences sometimes came into play as well

Each week there was some fluidity to who attended. The Aggie Network and the Aggie Nation is huge and has changed my life. Two other big things changed my life: First I met the Flints. So, they are in my "Top 5" of families. The other was going to A&M. On one hand, I have my Aggie ring and on the other, I have my wedding ring. That pretty much sums it up.

During my decade with our tailgate, I've never prioritized one over the other. My goal was to keep things balanced. You couldn't and shouldn't prioritize friends or family over coworkers or vice versa. If you set boundaries that are too strong, people read it and they won't come back. We wouldn't have been able to share with as many people as we did if our rules had been overly strict.

In social situations I don't have an agenda. It would limit me. I mask any anxiety of being in a big group by channeling that energy into running around and taking care of people I love.

Looking back, if I had had a specific agenda for the tailgates, that would have almost ruined it for me.

The first time we did a really big cook-off I felt guilty for not cooking all the food. I should have just let it happen. You don't have to stay up to 2:00 a.m. getting ready every single week. I like helping people, but so do others. Those are fun people to be around because you can be better together. People feel important and enjoy a situation more when they contribute.

I believe that in the tailgate and in life there are gardeners and flowers. Gardeners get things ready for the flowers. We had a lot of gardeners in our tailgate team. So the few flowers were good to go. If you couldn't contribute, you just didn't seem to fit in. By the end, literally, everyone brought something to the tailgating table via their role or responsibility.

Other things to understand about surrounding forces: You can't control the weather. You can't control the score. You can't control the traffic. You also can't control random tailgaters around you. You can't control the kickoff time. Listen, I get the rules of how college football has to be. However, as a tailgater, the 11:00 a.m. kickoff isn't my favorite.

In fact, the 11:00 a.m. kickoff versus the 6:00 p.m. kickoff is a polar-opposite day, depending on the season, how well the team is doing, and the other games scheduled on that day. I get it, but my personal preference is the 2:30 pm kickoff because it's the perfect balance, and it usually meant a bigger, better game. In some ways you're punished for losing: hello, 11:00 am kickoff. Bad team. Bad team. The 2:30 pm kickoff was my reward.

Sleep is optional for the 6:00 pm game because you're making it home with traffic and the trailer easily after midnight. But when you still find a way to enjoy it all, then you're in the right place with the right people.

Also, finding someone who knows how to grill is key. You don't want to make anyone sick. I always worried because I don't eat meat, so I never knew if it tasted good or if someone could get sick until it was too late. In the end, people who take care of each other and are willing to be flexible are the most enjoyable to be around.

Looking back: for the low-key games, we had a lot of family, friends, and fellow season ticket holders. For the big games, we had a lot more coworkers. At some point, people will come to the tailgate without even going to the game, which is when I realized that our tailgate had a culture because they didn't need the game. They needed the tailgate. We had created a community. What a compliment. What an experience. Thank you, cook-off team. Justin Brandenberger still talks about your ribs during lunch!

Beyond the Tailgate: You are the average of the five people you spend the most time around. There's no difference in that with regard to your relationships at home, at work, or at your tailgates. Communication is key. Tailgaters can't be responsible for what they don't know or can't see.

CHAPTER 3

❧

Earth, Wind, and Fire

Our View

Cheryl and I discuss the fundamental attribution error (FAE) from time to time. By definition, FAE means that people tend to unduly emphasize someone else's internal characteristics—such as character or intention—rather than external factors when explaining other people's behavior. This effect has been described as "the tendency to believe that what people do reflects who they are."[6]

For example, a coach who does not go for it on a 4th and 1 is blamed for his decisions based on the person *we* think they happen to be, not the situation. For example, society--or more specifically sports fans--may believe that a coach is "afraid" and playing not to lose. Conversely, when a coach goes for it on a 4th and 1, we think the coach is a "riverboat gambler" or "aggressive." When in reality, it's the situation that dictates the decision making. For example, the coach had a scorecard in his back pocket that said to go for it when he's on the opponents forty-five yard line. His field goal kicker is horrible from outside 50 yards and his top ranked defense can hold the other team should they fail to make the first. Most importantly, the offense's fullback is known for plowing through whatever is in front of him and to gain positive yardage. It's less the coach and more the situation. Even though, as a society, we like to ascribe the behavior to a person's internal characteristics. Whatever the internal drives or external factors, perception becomes reality.

How this plays out in real life can be quite compelling. Especially so when the games are close AND your team ends up on the short end of the scoreboard. ESPN's *College GameDay* came to town for the first of back-to-back night games at Kyle Field in 2016. The initial game pitted the at the time 8-1 Aggies against Oklahoma and the follow-up would be against Nebraska. We arrived early for the Oklahoma game and found a *great*, new tailgating spot—or so we thought.

The grass *was* greener than our traditional spot, *and* the new location had much, much more tailgating room. We could spread out a bit more and were closer to the stadium. The portable restrooms were nearby and clean. We thought we had found one of the best tailgating locations on campus. In the end, it took us two weeks to find out we were in the wrong spot

Late in the 4th quarter of a closely contested, hard-hitting game, Coach Dennis Franchione opted to kick a field goal on fourth and less than a yard—despite having a battering ram of a running back in Jorvorskie Lane available.

A monster of a man, the guy's nickname is "J-Train" because he favors a locomotive, and that's probably what it feels like when you try to tackle him.

The field goal cut the lead to one point.

On the other sideline and later in the fourth quarter, with about two minutes remaining, Oklahoma head football coach, Bob Stoops, choose a different path and went for it on 4th and 2 on his own side of the field *and* Oklahoma converted. The "twelfth man" at Kyle Field was oh so loud and the game oh so close, but a day and a tailgating location filled with promise ended on a solemn note and a one-point loss.[7]

A week later, we came back to the exact same tailgating spot.

Even though we thought we had found a new tailgating home. Unfortunately, the sick feeling from the week before returned when Texas A&M missed an extra point on an early touchdown that turned out to be the difference in the game. With 21 seconds left in the game Maurice Purify made a leaping, twisting catch on a pass from Zac Taylor to tie the game. The extra point won the game.

Normally after a game we stay at the tailgate to let the traffic clear out. Not this time. We broke down our equipment in record time and sat in the traffic—stunned by back-to-back one point losses. While we waited in the traffic, we all agreed that we would never set foot upon our "one-point loss" tailgate location ever again.

Whether you win or lose the game, there's much more to a situation. Your environment is key to your tailgate success and relationships. Typically, it is best to deal in the reality of the current situation. Differences abound, flexibility serves you well, karma matters and so too does the environment. Over the years, we've found that whether or not you are dealing with earth, wind, or fire, knowing your situation and giving others the benefit of the doubt by remembering the fundamental attribution error can ensure that you have a better time in your tailgating day, as well as your long-term relationships.

Earth

Have you ever seen the earth move? At one memorable tailgate, we experienced how rain can impact your day and then watched the stadium move. Not in the way that an earthquake would move you, but in the way that the student body engaged with the game. After watching a back-and-forth, triple-overtime contest that included rain, rainbows, and a victory, it was time to celebrate. If ever there was a moment to enjoy a tailgate, this was one of them.

Triple OT, Moving Stadiums and Rainbows – vs. Fresno State: 47-45 – Win

In what promised to be an uneventful game, the Bulldogs and Aggies battled in an overtime thriller. It happened to be the first tailgate where we encountered rain. We knew that a game plan for electronic equipment was important. We didn't lose any equipment, but we had to hustle. Thanks to the showers, a rainbow materialized over Kyle Field during the middle of the 3rd quarter.

Overtime games are rare enough, but triple OT plays out with so many twists and turns that it's incredible. As the overtimes progressed, the student body started moving back and forth across the top deck of Kyle Field to track the action. I've never seen anything like it before or since in terms of pure excitement.[8]

Wind

During a tailgate in 2011 on Labor Day weekend we encountered the wind. The Aggies were playing SMU and Tropical Storm Lee had passed well to the east of the Texas coastline, and, realistically, nowhere near College Station. However, as the storm meandered, the outer bands unexpectedly brought 35 mph winds gust to the tailgate. This also happened to be the year where massive rumors of the Aggies moving to the SEC had started. The winds of change were decidedly ushering in a new era of football.

Since it was the beginning of a new year, we decided it would be an appropriate time to bring a massive camp-out tailgate tent. Rather than using three or four 10' x 10' tents, we thought we'd be better off with a new, gigantic tent. As it turned out, the set up was incredibly difficult. We had a very handy tailgater help us tie down the tents. However, we soon realized we were at risk of being blown away and doubled down our efforts to secure our gargantuan monstrosity of a tent.

We took 2" x 10' orange ratchet straps and tied the tent down as tightly as possible. Too tight. As we took out all the slack, we effectively gave the tailgate tent no room to absorb a wind gust. Two of the ratchet straps were completely taut, and as we sought to ratchet down the third, we found out that with no room to be flexible, the metal framework on one of the legs effectively crumpled. Just like in life, too much tension in a turbulent environment created an unsustainable situation, and the structure collapsed.

It didn't ruin the day; it just meant we couldn't use the tent for the rest of the year. As we looked forward, we just reminded ourselves that the winds of change were around. A year later the games changed as the Aggies moved to the SEC.

You're Fired Up!

During a long day of tailgating it's easy to get a little fired up. People and the crowds tend to move a little faster and play a little harder when it's a big game. After one winning tailgate, the phrase made popular on *The Apprentice* came to light. "You're Fired!" wasn't just a catchphrase in this instance— Coach Dennis Franchione lost his job after one of our more memorable tailgates and victories.

Back-to-Back the Right Way – 38 to 30 – Win

Midway through the middle of the 2007 season we decided to provide an Aggie jersey to Cheryl for all the pregame meals and all the little things she did that added up to big things as she took care of the crew. We were hoping to give her the jersey on a game we thought we could win, but in an up-and-down season, we started to run out of dates.

As the final game approached, we discussed postponing the ceremony until the following year because we expected the

Longhorns—after having lost to us the prior year in Austin—to be sufficiently motivated to return the favor in College Station. It had been a long year for Coach Franchione—what with an email scandal and all. Many sports radio shows pontificated that the only way that Franchione could save his job was with a win over the #11 Longhorns, who were the heavy favorite as they rolled into Kyle Field.

Despite the ominous rainclouds hanging over the program and the stadium that day, the team presented the jersey in a pregame ceremony to Cheryl. We had a great tailgate and then walked over to the game expecting that it would be a long night. The game turned into a shocker and the jersey into a proverbial good luck charm. Ironically, on our way home we found out on the radio that Coach Fran—despite back-to-back wins over A&M's archrivals—had been fired.[9]

Cheryl's Thoughts

Weather is massive in the tailgating setting. Catastrophic events happen—between hurricanes and even the Bastrop County fires. Wind is probably the worst. The tents are meant for just about anything, but clearly not for that hurricane-force element.

You learn that when the ground is wet to put hay down so it doesn't get muddy. I do appreciate Doctor Neil Sanger and his game day forecasts for the Aggies.[10] He would actually tell you what was going on hour by hour before that was a thing. He helped you know what to plan for as best you could and is amazingly accurate.

You make adjustments. The electronics are always an issue when it's windy and wet. You can spend a lot of money replacing things if you aren't smart about it.

I choose to block out the cold and try to forget the "bad-weather games." One time we brought a heater to the tailgate and were so excited because it kept us warm. Neighboring tailgates came to appreciate the ideas and resourcefulness that our team brought to the table.

The hottest ones, though, have to be managed via three key words: Water. Water. Water.

On hot days things typically ended up being a sweaty mess, and many weekends were hot. Especially after the setup. Especially in September. Especially in Texas. Especially after hovering over food all day. People do dress up, and you should have some fashion sense. Lots of boots in Aggieland. All these combined to make for some long, hot tailgates.

Then I would look forward to the 70° days in October. The goal at our tailgates was to be comfortable. Some tailgates can become about fashion, but when you're uncomfortable, it does not work. In the end, you do you. Otherwise you'll be miserable—hot, cold, or otherwise.

Scatter shooting a bit on the "Earth, Wind, and Fire" title of this chapter made me think of the Bastrop fires and how everyone was late due to the traffic that one weekend.

You also want to get tarps and tie downs to block the wind and sun. You have to block the wind without creating a parachute that rips down your tents! You also want to situate the tents for the sun. The timing of the day also determines how you set up your day and how you set up your tailgate. Lots to do.

I do wonder how people tailgate in the snow. It would be fascinating to be in a tailgate in the snow, but I prefer the heat in Texas to snow anywhere. I would like to see how they do it though. We've tailgated in early October for the Notre Dame - Michigan game with the Allare family in South Bend. It was amazing, and it was chilly. Chilly but not snowing!

Beyond the Tailgate: Adapting, adjusting, and overcoming works as well in life as it does in tailgating. The winds of change are inevitable. Take note of what's happening and adjust. Whether you win the tailgate, the game or an argument there's always the potential of bringing too much stress to any situation. Let it go and play for another day.

CHAPTER 4

✿

Time Matters

"Dost thou love life? Then do not squander time, for that is the stuff life is made of."

—*Benjamin Franklin*

Our View

Being There for Your Others

There is a group of people that you will be readily available to in your tailgates and in your life. More specifically, you will become instantly available, thanks in large part to smart phones.

For example, they text; you respond. They call; you answer.

Some friends and families will engage repeatedly--taking you right up to the edge of annoyance; however, the key to your tailgate and your life is not only balance, but enjoyment of the experiences you share with your others. Do you have the right mix of family, friends, and tailgate friends? Are you enjoying the experience, or are you stressing out?

Let's consider the difference between friends and tailgate friends. In general, tailgate friends are more competitive with an intense Type A personality, and they typically have more of a rooting interest in the team you support at your tailgates. If you are a tailgater, you may not notice this as much initially because we like people who look and act like us. Note that this holds true with your group of friends beyond the tailgate, too, and that in all likelihood, if you are reading this book, that you meet the aforementioned characteristics. Or you are reading this book to better understand someone who has the aforementioned characteristics. Get ready, here we go!

To deliver some context. Break your tailgating crew into the following:

Family, which includes anyone you would see at a wedding, funeral, or family reunion. Sure, cousins sometimes act like friends or, more than likely, tailgate friends, but there's some value in knowing that you'll see this group of people during holidays and other big events. Strangely enough, I've found that it's good reputation management to communicate with this group even when they don't attend and routinely invite them to tailgate even if you know they can't make it. If you skip the invite or the courtesy follow-up text they can be the first to say negative things at family get-togethers. Keep them close and they will keep you close. You are family after all.

Friends, meaning the people who casually attend one or two tailgates per year. They like to have fun and enjoy spending time with you, but they aren't hard core into the program. Friends might show up for the big game and even ask you if you have extra tickets. They might not understand the magnitude of what's going on and, likely, value sports less than you or your tailgate friends do. These are great people to have around because your tailgate friends can occasionally be a bit intense.

Tailgate friends, the group who enjoys "the thrill of victory and the agony of defeat" and cares about the collegiate program or pro team in your life. You'll find a higher pregame attendance in this group, and they will be more willing to contribute to the greater good by donating time, energy, money, or equipment to the cause. If they can cook, that's a great addition, or if they know how to set up the satellite dish or get a generator going they can be a huge contributor.

Your best mix is to start with a foundation of approximately ten tailgate friends for optimal tailgating. Keep in mind that other than you and your spouse, there are no guarantees anyone will show up each week. And there's something to be said for that—the key being the knowledge that your spouse will show up with you. If you go too far too fast, you may find that your spouse might be left out, and for what it's worth, we don't recommend that—at all. In fact, we'd advise that if that's the scenario you are running into then you should consider attending other people's tailgates a few times a year and move smartly into the regular friends category. Tailgating is a team sport, and if you don't have the support at home for whatever reason, it's best to pass.

While you must assume—on a week-to-week basis—that your spouse will be there supporting you, you can't take it for granted. Having someone by your side for twelve hours of a during the tailgating experience is special, but it's not for every person or for every couple. I feel lucky to have shared a decade's worth of experiences with Cheryl. Moreover, whenever you do find that certain someone be sure to cherish each week and spend time together at the tailgate. There's plenty of time to spend time with and take care of others, but be sure to prioritize your spouse!

With one love of your life and ten tailgate friends you should be good to go. Then you can bring in 100+ other tailgaters from the friend category. Our top tailgate of all time was the aforementioned 2013 Alabama game. You will be there for everyone, but be there for your family first and foremost. Moreover, when making the difficult choice between Tailgate Crazy or Family Friendly, I recommend playing the long game and being Family Friendly. Family wins in the end, as no single tailgate or individual is worth the collateral damage.

Being There for Yourself

Somewhere along the way something changes. At first you will experience the sheer exhilaration of being part of something bigger than yourself. Shortly thereafter you receive the requisite dopamine and adrenaline shots based on the excitement you see in the eyes of the people and the outcomes of the games. This eventually is replaced with a feeling of "been there, done that." Somewhere near the third year of watching A&M play former Southwest Conference foes in the Big XII I ran into this feeling.

Exhilaration can be replaced by exhaustion. Then it hits you. Or at least it should. You can make the choice to have the entire experience energize you, or you can choose to let the entire experience drain you. It doesn't matter if you are an introvert or an extrovert or if you are a giver or a taker—the choice is yours. These things influence your feelings, but processing the information and the outcomes are well within your sphere of influence. Said another way: you can choose to own, recognize, and forgive behaviors and stay above the line. Or you can choose to ignore, deny, and lay blame for behaviors and work below the line. The line involves your intentions for the tailgate and really for all your relationships.

I travel extensively for business, and after an exhausting week of travel, I could choose to avoid all human contact, but there's nothing better than having the interaction of family, friends, and tailgaters to fuel my soul.

About five years in to the program I made the choice to take it to the next level by blogging for TailgatingIdeas.com. Founded by Dave Lamm, his website helped us test products, apply my writing skills, and improve upon some real-life search engine optimization (SEO) techniques. It also allowed me to secure cool new tailgating gear each year. Dave for encouraged and used my contributions and concepts, as well as product tests from our Texas-sized tailgates. Also as footnoted throughout, he's encouraged me to utilize portions of the blogs I've written throughout the years in the pages of this book. Dave captured a phenomenon as it was growing, and we helped to serve as a catalyst for even faster and meaningful growth.

Over the years, the tailgating and the blogging served as an outlet that's helped me become connected and to stay grounded. Additionally, it helped me learn how to be there more effectively for my wife.

Being There for Your Significant Other

If you think "time" does not matter, then read the review below and see what Cheryl said about the entire process for the tailgate in my September 2010 blog.

Winegard Carryout GM-1518: Tailgate Approved

You know that moment when you feel like you forgot something, but can't quite put your finger on it?

That's exactly what happened to me right after we set up our first two tailgates in 2010. I hadn't forgotten anything though. I was just missing the anxiety before and the stress after setting up our satellite TV feed.

The battle involved in triangulating the trio of coordinates for Tailgating TV is officially gone thanks to the ridiculously effective Winegard Carryout. Without hesitation the product is Tailgate Approved.

After real-world tailgating experiences this product now answers some questions that separate it from the traditional satellite dish setup. Here's a modified FAQ on the real world Winegard Carryout GM-1518 satellite setup for tailgating.

So, all you have to do is place the satellite within 5 degrees of level and it works. Really?

Our Texas A&M Tailgating area is on a slightly sloping hill just outside of Reed Arena across from Kyle Field on the corner of Kimbrough and Olsen.

Our natural setup for the Winegard was clearly not on level ground and probably not within 5 degrees of level. I eyeballed the unit, grabbed two paper napkins, stuffed the napkins under two of the three sides until it looked as level as level could be and continued on to the next step of connecting wires. That's all it took. It worked.

It's called a Portable Satellite Antenna, but can you move it?

During our first tailgate, right after the TV was up and running I was doing the proverbial celebratory victory lap in my mind and Cheryl shyly asked if we could move the Winegard to a more convenient location.

In years past I would have lost my patience and probably the signal—possibly each for the rest of the day. This time though, I shrugged my shoulders and said, "Why not? Let's find out."

She moved the Winegard about a foot. It—of course—lost its signal. The satellite antenna then began to crank, whiz and whir its way back into place. In less than a minute the Notre Dame vs. Purdue game was back on the television. Really, pretty amazing.

Does the product need to be elevated to avoid signal interference from foot traffic?

From a commonsense perspective I wasn't willing to leave the unit on the ground to test the theory; however, we did elevate the unit three to four feet off the ground inasmuch as we placed the Winegard off the ground on a table next to the television. Then we tested the reception at the higher level by having several of our tailgaters walk right past the unit at a casual gait.

Our test and the rest of the foot traffic during the day didn't interfere with the TV reception at all.

Come on . . . How long does it really, really take to set up?

Total work time: two minutes. Total time to enjoying college football games: 12-15 minutes.

It takes longer for the satellite to download the programming information from Dish Network than it does for the satellite to lock on the correct coordinates.

Connecting the coaxial cables and the RCA cables takes about two minutes. It takes another five for the satellite to lock and then another five to eight minutes for the programming information from Dish Network to fully integrate—depending on how long it's been since you've last uploaded the programming. All told 12 -15 minutes. Keep in mind though you're not doing anything during the last ten.

The setup is so much faster and simpler than the traditional satellite dish, it's hard to fathom. Like the year that you picked up Kurt Warner off the waiver wires and he took the Rams and your fantasy team to the championship. It's almost too good to be true.

Can you change the color of the dome?

Say what you will, but I believe that the white dome needs to have a little more of the Spirit of Aggieland in it. So, we have plans to paint the Winegard maroon before our next tailgate.

I've been told by company representatives that I will void the warranty when and if I paint the dome.

It's the same thing I heard from Apple about unlocking the iPhone. However, the people that I know that unlocked their iPhones actually enjoyed the product more. The same thing will hold true with the Carryout in my estimation.

The game plan is to spray paint the dome with maroon, non-lead-based paint.

Final Thought

Cheryl, my wife, and I are looking around. The TV is working. The Tailgate is set. Everything's done. We've got time on our hands. The weather is beautiful. Family and friends are all around. Stress level is down.

'Hey,' she said. 'Put this in your blog. Winegard gave me my husband back.'"[11]

Ultimately, "time" is what you spending with people in your life.

In all that you do to take care of others and in all that you do to take care of your family please keep in mind the importance of taking care of your spouse. Spending time with each other is one of the most underestimated, yet important aspects of tailgating. Over time, we traded in our divide and conquer approach for spending time together. Instead of Cheryl preparing the meals and me loading the trailer—which is what we did at the beginning—I started to help out in the kitchen, and she pitched in with loading and unloading the trailer. In today's society, time is the precious commodity we're all looking to find. Spend as much as possible with those you care about the most—not the other way around. That common time spent together should help you develop a positive shared history during each weekend of tailgating.

Cheryl's Thoughts

You've got to be ready. To be there for others you pretty much have to be there first--mentally and physically. If someone is coming early to help you set up, you have to be present. Thank you friends, thank you friends for the years of helping us set up and tear down, espe-cially on the set-up.

Heads up--some people and family do expect a tailgate to be set up for them. The set-up and tear-down people are the ones I appreciate in ways I can't explain. Did you get that from the above? The cooperation and teamwork and communication was and still is amazing.

If there's traffic or if the parking lot's full you can't just drop stuff off. Early in tailgating is better.

We learned a few divide-and-conquer approaches throughout the years that did NOT work out. One of our least favorite tailgates was when Jim and I left the house in different cars. I was caught in traffic with my passengers due to an accident on the highway. We were fine, just stuck in traffic and arrived about an hour later than they did. However, we had the food. That was stressful, and we don't separate now for trips for whatever reason. Couples are better together.

Also, know that some people believe in arriving fashionably late. That's okay for some, but not so good for your tailgate team and in particular for the set-up team. My mind-set was: *Let's set up, and then we can choose to be flexible.*

Teachers maintain flexibility quite well. You have your plan teaching science with supplies and equipment and then something random happens that day to throw off your meticulous planning.

Plan for the best. Prepare for the worst. Expect somewhere in the middle.

During the amazing Alabama tailgate, we had to go into overdrive because we had 25 to 35 more people than expected show up, and it was incredibly hot. A 95° day made it tough, and no wind made the air stale and humid. We ran out of water. We unplugged the Jägermeister machine and asked late arrivers to bring in liquid reinforcements of the most basic kind. During tailgates you cannot leave and return, nor would you want to. So, texting those late arrivers and having them bring you whatever you are missing or about to run out of is a key to success.

In terms of spending time together one of my favorite times of the tailgating day was the drive up and the drive back. As the driver I would think of questions all day long knowing that I could direct question games on the way home for a little extra fun. The questions I'd ask were silly to serious. The following is a list of questions I remember asking over the years. Try it on your next long trip!

- your favorite sports movie?
- best family memory?
- favorite cartoon character?
- worst fear?
- favorite part of your week?
- the last dream you had?
- the scariest movie you've seen?
- the superhero you are most like?
- favorite game?
- favorite tailgate?
- favorite pet?
- favorite teacher?

It's endless really. And you want to ask "Why?" after. Not to put people on the defensive, but in order to encourage them to share their stories. The corresponding conversations strengthened the bonds that come from people who really share themselves and open up to the opportunity to connect. It's interesting too. People really do put down their phones to listen to others share the stories of their lives.

The tailgates allowed, and maybe even encouraged, people to take the time to share the stories of their lives, the day or maybe even just their week. Tailgates set the stage to spend great time with great people.

People would stop by our tailgates and not go to the other tailgates they were supposed to go to because they were getting to hear the stories of everyone's lives. People were literally having the time of their lives and getting to tell everyone about it.

Beyond the Tailgate: The time you spend with others is valuable. Honest. Real. The conversations are the most fun. Find ways to connect with your spouse, your family, your friends, and yourself. Spend time with your tailgate friends, too, knowing that all of the experiences will help energize you and those around you.

CHAPTER 5

❧

Feed the Forces

"Food is our common ground, a universal experience."

—*James Beard, legendary chef and food writer*

Our View

Our first tailgates started with lawn chairs and coolers. It wasn't until much later that we evolved into snacks much less to a full-on cook team. In fact, for a time in the middle of our decade-plus run, it seemed that we were poised to be more "technological tailgaters" than "food connoisseurs."

Notwithstanding the Winegard Carryout HDTV setup and the two 60-inch TVs, we were creative with our technology. One year we had an Xbox where we would play the game being played on one TV in a video game. Meanwhile, the same game was actually on the second TV. It was fun for the gamers among us. We also had times when we decorated the tailgates during the holiday season with festive lights.

The evolution of the food, though, was where we took things to the next level. During the early years, we more or less had a "bring your own food" philosophy. However, as the tailgate grew, we brought small cooking grills. So small that you could imagine cooking only three hamburgers at a time--really small. At the time, though, they were the best-tasting hamburgers ever. We enjoyed our progress in the moment.

One of our tailgaters, Matty Ice, would set up the grill and keep the hamburgers and hot dogs coming. At the same time, we moved into chips, dips, and deli meats and used seasonality to help bring us into new, more versatile places with our menus. One cold winter day we made sure to serve chili because, well, it was one of the items we needed to review for the Tailgating Ideas blog. Here's the review and the recipe. With more, additional family recipes to follow.

As tailgating moves further into the fall and the temperatures in Texas turn cooler, there's nothing better than chili to help keep your tailgate warm.

After tailgate testing Cin Chili, we found it to be such a perfect match that we adjusted our future menus to include Cin Chili for the last three tailgates of the season.

Cin Chili is a family owned business started by Cindy Reed Wilkins. With two first place trophies from the Terlingua International Chili Championship, Cindy is the only person with back-to-back titles in the history of the competition. She's the Archie Griffin of chili cook-offs, if you will. Griffin, a former running back for Ohio State University, is the first and only consecutive winner of the Heisman Trophy.

After years of perfecting her recipe—she's won more than 300 cook-offs in her career—Cindy now shares her chili recipes and spices with those interested. She's even appeared on the Food Network's *Throwdown with Bobby Flay*. Flay routinely challenges the absolute masters in different areas of cooking expertise like BBQ, pizza, and chili. When it came time to take on the world's best in chili, he went to Cindy's door.

The Cin Chili mix is value priced at $5. Ingredients include all the usual suspects: red pepper, jalapeno pepper, salt, and special chili powders.

Cin Chili is spicy enough to keep your mouth watering and the drinks flowing, but it's not so hot that you need to call the fire department. A genuine mix of chili goodness from one of the all-time greats, Cindy Reed Wilkins.

Cin Chili Is Tailgate Approved

The recipe below serves ten.

Cin-Chili Chili

> 2 pounds stew beef
> 1 teaspoon vegetable oil
> 4 1/2 tablespoons chili powder – divided use
> 5 teaspoons garlic powder – divided use
> 1 (8 oz.) can tomato sauce
> 1 1/2 cups beef broth
> 1 teaspoon chicken base or bouillon granules
> 1 jalapeño, seeded and chopped
> 1 tablespoon onion powder
> 1/2 teaspoon cayenne pepper
> 1 1/2 teaspoons white pepper – divided use
> 2 cups water

1/2 teaspoon salt
2 green chili peppers
1 tablespoon paprika
1 tablespoon Italian seasoning
1 teaspoon onion powder
2 teaspoons ground cumin
1/8 teaspoon salt

In a heavy kettle, brown stew beef in oil. Stir in 1 tablespoon chili powder and 2 teaspoons garlic powder.

In a large bowl, combine tomato sauce, beef broth, chicken base, chopped jalapeno, 1 tablespoon onion powder, 2 teaspoons garlic powder, cayenne pepper, 1 teaspoon white pepper, water, 1 tablespoon chili powder, salt, and green chili peppers. Add to the beef mixture and stir. Bring to a boil, reduce the heat, and simmer for 1 1/2 hours.

Meanwhile, in a small bowl, combine paprika, Italian seasoning, 1 teaspoon onion powder, 1 teaspoon garlic powder, 1/2 teaspoon white pepper, and 2 1/2 tablespoons chili powder. Add to the beef mixture, adding more beef broth or water if too thick. Remove the green chili peppers and simmer for 20 minutes. Stir in cumin and salt. Simmer for 10 minute.[12]

A few great family, yet healthy recipes for our tailgates included Cheryl's queso as well as her spinach and artichoke dip. You won't be disappointed!

Cheryl's Queso, a crowd favorite

> 1 (64 oz. package of) Velveeta, chopped into small chunks
>
> 2 cans of Campbell's Nacho Cheese soup
>
> 2 cans of RO*TEL Mexican Style Diced Tomatoes with Lime Juice and Cilantro. Drain and mix
>
> Put Crock-pot on low until queso simmers, or microwave 4 to 5 minutes and stir.
>
> For meat lovers, add cooked ground beef or chorizo.
>
> For health nuts, use light Velveeta and eliminate Nacho Cheese soup from the recipe. One fun tailgate concept is to share recipes and name them after the other team. This could be the "Artich-Oklahoma" Spinach Dip for example!

Cheryl'sArtichoke Spinach Dip, a healthy alternative to the original. For a big pan of artichoke dip:

> Preheat oven to 350°
>
> 3 (10 oz. packages frozen creamed spinach, thawed
>
> 2 (14 oz. cans artichoke hearts, drained and chopped
>
> 3½ cups of mozzarella cheese, shredded
>
> 2½ cups of Parmesan cheese, shredded

1 teaspoon of fresh lemon juice

crushed red pepper to taste

Combine all the ingredients except for parmesan cheese and blend thoroughly

Place in an oven-proof dish, and top with Parmesan cheese. Cover and bake an hour at 350° until hot and bubbly.

Serve with your favorite chips for your favorite tailgaters. Mmmmm good.

Another fan favorite that's made it to almost every tailgate.

Cheryl's 7-Point Spread Tailgate Dip

1 (1 oz.) package taco seasoning mix

2 (16 oz.) cans of refried beans

1 (8 oz.) package cream cheese, softened

1 (16 oz.) container of sour cream

3 cups of guacamole

1 large tomato, chopped

1 bunch chopped green onions

1 small head iceberg lettuce, shredded

1 (6 oz.) can sliced black olives, drained

2 cups shredded Mexican blend cheese

Mild jalapeños (optional)

In a medium bowl, blend the taco seasoning mix and refried beans. Spread the mixture onto a large serving platter. Mix the sour cream and cream cheese in a medium bowl. Spread over the refried beans. Add the next layer by spreading the guacamole over the cream mix. Place a layer of tomato, green onions, and lettuce over the guacamole. Top with Cheddar cheese. Garnish with black olives and jalapeños as desired.

I find it easiest to add the cheese, olives, and jalapeños right before serving.

Cheryl also always makes a great guacamole mix.

Cheryl's Guacamole

4 or 5 ripe quality avocados

2 (12 oz.) cans of RO*TEL Mexican Style Diced Tomatoes with Lime Juice and Cilantro, drained

Mash the avocadoes until there are no chunks. Add in the drained RO*TEL and 2 tablespoons of sour cream. Stir. Add salt, pepper, garlic powder, and lime to taste.

Serve with desired chips.

Tailgate warning: One of the unexpected consequences of our advances in the food space was the use of our Honda A2000 generator. For those not well versed in the space, the 2000 stands for the wattage you can pull from the different pieces of electronic equipment that you utilize during the tailgate.

To give you an idea: we were used to a 60-inch TV pulling somewhere near 100 watts of energy. During the day we would run current for TVs, cable boxes, radios, and even iPhone chargers without much ado; however, the day we plugged in a new Crock-Pot, we blew the circuit. Bam! No college football games for the rest of that day. The older Crock-Pot that we had been using pulled 750 watts, and with the TVs, the portable satellite, video games, holiday lights, and electrical equipment, we had just pushed our generator to its literal limits. The new Crock-Pot turned out to be much more than we bargained for on the circuits that we were utilizing.

Over the next several years we were able to cover off on all the equipment and even introduced a hot dog machine, of all things—like the ones you'd find at 7-Eleven that cooks and rotates the hotdogs—as well as a heat-generating nacho machine and a Jägermeister shot chiller machine. From hot to cold we had the range of food possibilities covered!

One week after the Crock-Pot snafu we purchased another A2000 generator, and all the electrical charges that we needed to consider were much more carefully calculated. Moving forward the details for the wattage resided right next to a chart we printed out that served as our guide for the football games that we wanted to watch each weekend.

The Indispensable College Football TV Schedule Link

Getting ready to head out to a college football tailgate, but not quite sure which games are on? Over the last several years I've found this link to be unbelievably useful: http://lsufootball.net/tvschedule.htm

Normally a website wouldn't be worthy of an article, but in this case the link is so useful and so on point that it's worth the proverbial tip of the tailgating cap.

It stands to reason the link would come from LSU where they take their tailgating very seriously, but what makes this site so good? The schedule not only updates regularly, but the webmaster provides some very nice touches in the form of printable schedules for Direct TV owners.

While I'm a Dish Network guy it's still a great option to have. The site isn't particularly fancy, but the devil is in the details, and this site nails down the times, networks, and channels without fail.

You can best use the site by taking action before you leave the house. On game day print out the sheet before you depart. Then when you arrive, get the TV up and running at the tailgate and hand the remote control along with the list of the day's games to one of your buddies. With that you'll definitely get the tailgating day off on the right foot.

As you move into October, where the kickoff times for most of the Division I Football Bowl Subdivision (FBS) games are still up in the air due to TV's heavy influence, I've found this link to be more consistently reliable than many conference sites.

Take a look around, print out the sheet on your way out the door and enjoy your college football tailgate.[13]

As we moved into the next phase of our "food for the forces" concept we, thankfully, ran into like-minded tailgaters. John Burr and John Montgomery helped take our tailgating to the next level in terms of setting up meetings with sponsors and helping our tailgate cook team—also known as the Cowboy Mardi Gras Cookers—make our tailgate one of the best places to be in all of Aggieland. The team routinely competes in the Houston Livestock Show and Rodeo BBQ cook-off. For those who have not been to the event, the rodeo houses the World's Championship BBQ Contest on the grounds of NRG park on the Thursday, Friday, and Saturday before the livestock show begins. More than 250 teams compete to be recognized for their creations that must be cooked on a wood fire.[14]

The Cowboy Mardi Gras Cookers routinely prepare some of the most amazing food. Whether it involved chicken, brisket, ribs, or mashed potatoes it was routinely incredible.

With a 20-foot trailer-hitched, fire-grilled cook machine, the team had to be in place no later than the night before the game to ensure that the meats were properly prepared. The coordination and menu preparation takes immense planning and coordination. Thanks to, Cheryl, as well as John Burr, John Montgomery, and their entire team for being such an incredible part of the Varsity Tailgaters tailgate team through the years.

The other lasting memory of the tailgating food scene was Cheryl's willingness to give to others. This holds true every weekend, but especially so when we closed in on the Thanksgiving holiday each year. Whether a game against our former rivals or LSU, we often shared the task of putting together more than 200 bacon-wrapped doves in our home. The process involved separating the doves into bite-sized chunks that allows for a bit of Philadelphia cream cheese, some jalapeno, all in a lean bacon wrap around the doves that we grilled.

Putting together 200 of these on the Wednesday night before Thanksgiving many years in a row resulted in so many happy tailgaters on Thursday. It's remarkable. And I smile as I look back and think about those late nights we spent together. Remarkable what you can do together for the greater good!

Cheryl's Thoughts

The menu matters, and I have the tendency to think of each tailgate as Thanksgiving.

I have more fun finding pictures of the food to send to people. I loved doing and planning the food more than anything. It's a labor of love. My love language. It's a lot like the love of the game for many and where I contribute the most.

Sometimes I might make too much of something that I thought would be good. Veggie and fruits were great early on, but the grilled bacon-wrapped doves have been, by far, the most popular. That's mostly later in the year though; during the season, we had more of a chips-and-queso crowd. Interestingly, hours of vegetable preparation were replaced by ten minutes of queso prep, which was a better use of time and the crowd was happier. Simpler was better.

Getting cold cuts, cheese, and bread was popular when we were not grilling. The more simplicity in the foods allowed people to contribute more too. Complexity makes for fewer contributors. When people—who enjoy competition—can contribute to the greater good, it brings people closer. People would share recipes through food or contribute via a really nice bottle of wine. They would share family stories, too, which everyone loved.

Chicken wings were popular, too. I suppose this was also a meat-and-potatoes kind of crowd. And then we progressed to a place with the cook team where the love language included cooking all day. Sometimes the cook off team couldn't BBQ, so others would bring smaller items like hot dogs or burgers. It all worked so well together in retrospect.

One of my favorite memories was when we first did bacon-wrapped doves and let the group know via email. The responses people gave us were amazing and were only superseded by the experiences we shared in person.

With hundreds of bacon-wrapped doves prepared on a Green Egg and cooked well into the morning, the reality was that there was no way—seemingly—that our crew would eat them all. But they did and still do. Every year. Every time. Here's a recipe for the bacn-wrapped dove fans in the crowd!

Bacon-Wrapped Dove, Quail, or Pheasant

Dove, quail, and/or pheasant cut into 1.5 to 2.0 inches per piece

Philadelphia Cream Cheese

Tamed Mezzetta jalapeno peppers--but be careful! We like spicy, and this is just the right amount for people who might have ulcers or other sensitive digestive tracts. You have to think of everyone when you feed a whole team.

Bacon

Toothpicks--Soak toothpicks in water for easier insertion and to make the cooking process a little less fire oriented.

Put a teaspoon of cream cheese and one jalapeno on the bird pieces. Curl the bird. Wrap the bacon around the bird. Add a toothpick or two to hold items in place.

Marinate overnight in an olive oil, balsamic vinaigrette, crackled pepper, and a sea salt mix. As a Plan B: you could simply use an Italian salad dressing.

Smoke the wrapped birds in a Green Egg on game day at 400° with mesquite chips to bake in the flavor.

Grill the dove breasts for three to four minutes on each side. When you are finished, the breast should be brown and the bacon crispy. Some bacon searing is a nice touch.

Also, I'd recommend that you become creative with your food selection for tailgates. After a trip to Spain we had a "tapas tailgate."

The best tailgates, for me, have been on Thanksgiving. I remember making cranberries and oranges once. I also remember one of the last Thanksgivings when LSU actually played TAMU on Thanksgiving Day. We fried turkeys. It was scary because of what can happen if you dip a frozen turkey into the fryer: It can explode, but the team thankfully had it handled.

Beyond the Tailgate: People gather for food. Share the best food and the best experiences. You learn a lot about grilling, cooking, and each other. Along the way the tailgate helped me take cooking from the place of being a chore or responsibility to being a love language for Cheryl. She was also thankful when people offered blessings and when we had family, friends, neighbors, and associates around the tailgate. That was a blessing in and of itself.

CHAPTER 6

≫

Inside or Out: To Ticket or Tailgate

"Joy: *[voice over]* These are Riley's memories. And they are mostly happy if you'll notice, not to brag. But the really im-portant ones are over here.

Joy: *[voice over]* I don't want to get too technical, but these are called core memories. Each one came from a super important time in Riley's life. Like when she first scored a goal. It was so amazing."[15]

—*Inside Out: The Mind of Riley Anderson*

Our View

One of the core memories I have from our tailgating days is a play from inside Kyle Field when #1 Alabama played #6 Texas A&M on September 14, 2013. The year before, on the way to a Heisman-trophy run, Johnny Football and the Aggies upset the then #1 ranked Crimson Tide. This game was the rematch.

Down 42-28 in the fourth quarter, the Aggie defense created and recovered a fumble when it appeared Alabama was going to score a touchdown and close out the game. Pinned on their own five-yard line, Manziel threw a pass from deep in the Aggies end zone that resulted in a 95-yard touchdown pass to Michael Evans. It cut the lead to seven points. Without a doubt, Kyle Field achieved one of its all-time loudest moments in history. If the stadium had had a roof, it would have erupted on that play.

One of the greatest changes that happened when the Aggies made the jump to the SEC was the tailgating scene. The biggest news for Aggies was the likelihood that—just like the Alabama game—there would be huge numbers of people outside the stadium versus inside the stadium much more often.

Jim depicted this in a blog in August of 2011--the year before the team made the jump to the new conference.[16]

Texas A&M SEC Tailgating Guide

Welcome to the new league Aggies. Things are about to change on the tailgating landscape. Let's take a look at some of the key differences that will occur upon Texas A&M's arrival in the Southeastern Conference.

Tailgating Presence Will Increase Outside of the Stadium

The Aggies are preseason #8 for football this year. With the new SEC excitement, the tailgating intensity will only go up. There will be more tailgating done outside the stadium once the Aggies join the SEC.

At Texas A&M there are those that tailgate outside the stadium during the game, but many times, tailgaters that are just hanging out are lucky enough to be offered an extra seat for games like SMU or Idaho.

That scenario will change considerably when LSU, Alabama, and Ole Miss come to town. In fact, for the first couple of years, even Vanderbilt and Kentucky will create enough intrigue that tickets will become even more precious. As a result, the tailgating outside of Kyle Field will grow, and Texas A&M will start to show up more often on Top Ten Tailgating Lists.

More Opposing School Colors

School colors will be even more prevalent and prominent. I predict that there will be LSU tailgaters at Kyle Field during the entire season once the SEC deal is inked.

This year, even though LSU and Mississippi State were not among the eight teams playing in the College World Series, their fans were in full effect with full-on tailgates running outside of the stadium in Omaha. I know because we attended College World Series games in 2011, 2014 and 2016.

As such, some enterprising Tigers will possibly have their gold and purple tents up and active for the entire season at Kyle Field. The LSU fans just don't care what anyone else thinks of them. With their Cajun heritage and strong Houston presence they'll rationalize that it's just them getting ready and pre-gaming for when the Aggies and Tigers play--even if it's weeks out.

Thank God for Starkville though. At least at Mississippi State games the school colors will be the same and the in your face antics will be much less likely.

Texas A&M tailgaters are a welcoming group. SEC schools? Not so much.

More Trash Talking @ Tailgates Than Ever Before

Despite A&M's good nature, there will likely be more conflict in the tailgating parking lots than ever before. In large part it will be due to A&M being the new kids on the SEC block, and the fact that many of the current SEC schools aren't afraid to get in each other's faces. It almost seems to be a sign of tough love in these states. SEC schools support each other when they are playing out of conference, but when it's head-to-head—it's game on!

At an LSU versus Florida game I attended in October of 2006 with Jim Moran and Pam LeJeune, Tiger fans were in the faces of anyone wearing Florida blue—yelling "Gator Bait." Moreover, LSU fans walked around with a Florida player hanging in effigy. The whole tradition of hanging the other team's mascot in effigy is a new play for the Aggies. It's something that we'll have to get used to for away games.

A New Level of Intensity

In fact, one of the biggest tailgating differences is that in many SEC towns like Oxford and Tuscaloosa, there aren't any professional teams nearby.

The net effect? Aggie passion and attendance are considerably compromised by tailgaters that spend their money and tailgating time about 90 miles south in Houston with the Texans or three hours north with the Cowboys.

When There Is Less to Do, Football Matters More

Head Coach Dennis Franchione is a great example. After a successful run at TCU, Coach Fran landed at Alabama for two years. He left quickly. Or was he run out of town? He landed at Texas A&M where he headed up the program for a very long four years.

Just like the scenario with Coach Fran, the Aggies are a patient bunch. With Alabama and the SEC, it's more direct. Roll Tide or Roll on Out of here.

Longhorn Changes

The one downside to Texas A&M's move to the SEC is the ending of an historic relationship with the team from Austin. When the Aggies join the SEC, a huge tradition will come to an end.

Truly, this will be the last year of the game thanks in large part to the creation of the Longhorn Network.

It's going to take some adjusting. In between every quarter of every game, the Aggies sing a fight song about the their soon to be former rivals. It's already interesting enough that this happens when Texas A&M plays other teams, but I can't quite imagine what it will be like when the Aggies don't play them at all.

From a tailgating perspective a former rival's absence will take a little edge out of the Thanksgiving Tailgate experience and the rumors habitually fly about possible replacements and rescheduling on both sides. Some believe that Texas is working behind the scenes to schedule a Notre Dame night game on Thanksgiving Day.

Who should the Aggies play? Well Alabama has Auburn. LSU plays Arkansas. It would be great if the Aggies . . . the 13th SEC team played the 14th SEC team. If that's Florida State, then that would be great; however, games against Virginia Tech or North Carolina seem less appealing. Either way that change will be a big one for many families across the state of Texas and the game day tailgating experience. Note: It became LSU.

The series will surely end though. Texas A&M, after playing a brutal SEC schedule, does not need an emotional, high degree of difficulty game to bolster any national rankings. Moreover, with upcoming high-profile, non-conference home and away games scheduled by the Aggies it is unlikely that the Aggies would put them on the schedule for at least a decade.

Although regular season games are unlikely, I can see a scenario where an SEC Aggie team plays a Big XII champion team in the Cotton Bowl in Dallas or at the Sugar Bowl in New Orleans at some point down the line. A prerequisite would be that each team would have at least ten wins in the same season

Even though the campuses are just over 100 miles apart, an Aggie move to the SEC will make the distance between Austin and College Station insurmountable. Ultimately, this will lead to the biggest tailgating change of all when both schools will say goodbye for the foreseeable future via one last Texas-sized tailgate on Thanksgiving Day in November of 2011.

Two years later, after the prediction, the unimaginable had already become true. No more games versus the arch rivals and in only the second year of the new conference A&M Tailgate coordinator Neil Peltier advised, before the aforementioned Alabama game, that: 'We could easily see 90,000 [inside] Kyle and close to the same tailgating outside.'

The Alabama versus Texas A&M rematch was the equivalent of a college Super Bowl and the reported numbers turned out be bigger that Peltier's estimate.[17]

A Core Memory

Closing in on our 25th wedding anniversary, I think our conversation about the Alabama versus Texas A&M game in 2013 was an important one. Call it a core memory. While not a recorded transcript, the gist of the conversation went something like this:

> Jim: Hey, based on RSVPs, we're going to have 200+
>
> at the tail-gate this weekend.
>
> Cheryl: Oh, that's all.
>
> Jim: Crazy question: do you want to go to the game?

Cheryl: Well, would you want to skip the game and manage the tailgate?

Jim: We could sell the tickets?

Cheryl: No.

Jim: Well we started all this to go to games like this one, right?

Cheryl: When I was in school I couldn't afford to go to the games. I remember working in Heldenfels Learning Resource Center during the games to help pay for school.

Jim: I remember.

Cheryl: Can the team manage the tailgate?

Jim: I think so. I hope so. I'm pretty sure. They'll be fine.

Cheryl: Then let's go to the game.

Jim: Awesome. Let's go to the game. We'll be there early and stay late.

As you know from the chapter opening, we did go to the game, and I'd love to tell you that the Aggies won that day and the Varsity Tailgaters had a flawless day underneath sun-kissed 72° weather. However, we did develop a positive shared history and some classic stories about the game and an overall amazing experience. Unfortunately, the Aggies lost; we weathered a 95°, no-wind day; and we had a few tailgaters who celebrated the occasion a little too aggressively.

One group of friends got into a wrestling match. It was friendly at first, but a few people got nervous as the match escalated between two revelers amongst our group of friends. As one tailgater said: "It was kind of cool at first, then kind of edgy, and then it stopped. Thank goodness, it stopped."

One of our tailgaters had a little too much to drink when their inner entrepreneur arrived in the form of him selling Sarah's Famous Cookies to people passing by on behalf of her charity. The charity part–Beau Means Business[18]—was sincere and considerable donations were made, but at that given moment in time he may not have been the best representative given his inebriated state.

Overall, the overwhelming majority had a great time, and we shared the human condition. We were building a rich, powerful, shared, positive history with family and friends.

Cheryl's Thoughts

Huge stress. At first I thought I was supposed to get tickets for our group, but people were quite content to stay at the tailgate. It was a little stressful with family too. We didn't want to disappoint people. My immediate family is so "last minute."

While I recognize some people were perfectly content to watch the game from the tailgate. I actually wanted to go to the games. My preference is to see the Fightin' Texas Aggie band. My memories of listening to them practice while I was in school at TAMU, living in Keathley Hall, gets reactivated each time I hear them play.

Sometimes at a tailgate I felt bad about going into the game when other people couldn't get tickets. The TV was a big draw, but also having free food and drinks. TAMU did not sell alcohol in stadium until after the rebuild. As such, lots of people were—shall I say—more excitable later in the day. Mostly good times. Before the game and after the game were really two separate experiences, and a lot depended on the outcome of the game.

After watching a game for four hours and coming back there was even more celebration to be had—especially, even though it didn't matter to me--when the Aggies won.

It was, for certain games, almost like seeing the same crew post game who was so excited to see you before the game. In years where TAMU was winning, we had so much fun.

Also, as far as tickets go, you have to make budget decisions. Everyone, eventually, wants to retire, so you can't buy tickets for everyone. I knew it was okay, about seven years in, when people had given us extra tickets that we could *not* giveaway while at the tailgate.

People preferred to share their days and experiences at the tailgate!

Beyond the Tailgate: Are you inside or outside? Go inside and enjoy the shared experiences.

CHAPTER 7

✿

Potluck

"Oh, you forgot to RSVP? Well there won't be any cake for
you. Or a seat. Or a meal. Are you starting to see the pattern
here?"

—*Anonymous wedding quote*

Our View

Unlike the Alabama game, and as you'll read in more detail
in "Chapter 9 - Beyond the Bandwagon", we only received
forty RSVPs for one of our popular Tenth Anniversary tailgates;
however, more than 120 people showed up. With attendance
three times more than what we had planned for, we knew we
were in trouble. We ran out of food and started to run out of
drinks. And to make matters worse Ole Miss and more than
150,000 fans were coming to Kyle Field the next weekend.
Moreover, my sister, Cindy Christian, and her boys and our
nephews, Flint and Philip, would be joining us. Add our
wonderful brother-in-law Andrew into the mix and all the
conversation about how amazing tailgating is at the grove in

Oxford, and we quickly realized that it was time to bring some additional coordination to the chaos. The tailgate had become unmanageable so we made key adjustments. Over the years we've:

- added a Wells-Cargo trailer;
- introduced a wristband system;
- added a requirement to either help set up or break down the tailgate for all access. Essentially meaning all the food and drink you could handle;
- established a standard fee if you did not set up or break down the tailgate in order to secure all access to the tailgate. There was a need to offset food costs, TV subscription costs, ice costs, gasoline costs, and people who wanted to take more than give. Moreover, some people preferred to contribute financially; and
- secured sponsors that connected to our core group of tailgaters.

Additionally, we identified the menu plans and needs the week before each game to arrive with just a little bit more than what we thought we might need. To stay connected and be on the safe side, Cheryl coordinated this with family and friends. Many people loved the concept of bringing food or drinks. We just kept encouraging people to bring something, anything that contributed to the greater good.

One family brought utensils and napkins each week. It was a great addition and much needed. It seems simple, but every contribution counts. Details like trash bags had to be attended too as well. Every detail matters.

The Land Grab

One of the more interesting elements that evolved over time was the need to secure the "land grab" before the tailgate setup officially began each year *and* at some level each week. As I mentioned in Chapter 1, we eventually moved from the back part of campus to one of the, if not *the*, premier locations—on the corner of Kimbrough and Olson—with tens of thousands of passersby each game.

The way the system works in Aggieland, university officials —or were they tailgate officials?—blew an air horn at noon on Fridays. This horn serves the purpose of letting everyone know they could stake their claim to their land and actually begin the process of setting up their tailgates. Initially, I enjoyed taking off Fridays of Labor Day weekends to make sure that we were properly positioned going into each season. A few friends traveled with me, and we had a great time meeting and greeting the other excited tailgaters. In fact, as you built relationships with those around you, you began supporting and protecting each other's particular parcel of land. It takes a village and in some ways we were building our own weekend neighborhoods.

As we moved through the years, we consistently upgraded our position and made sure to get the support of those around us. Fundamentally, once you lock into your location for the first tailgate, it establishes your position for the rest of the year. The first weekend is typically key, and in many years we were the first to arrive. However, the following weeks still required support.

Ironically, one of our best tailgaters happened to be Josh K., who had been one of Mrs. Flint's students in eighth grade and now joined us as a junior in college!

Moreover, Josh's dad, Gary K., was Cheryl's boss—as the principal--at one of the schools that she worked in for several years. It is a very small world, and your tailgate family will extend into places and situations that you cannot even imagine.

Josh was a passionate Aggie, and he took over the Friday morning air horn land grab during the SEC seasons. After the horn blew, he would take a few stakes and tie down our area. Then he would place a few of our 10' x 10' tents there and head back to class. It might sound simple in concept, but it took some discipline to execute consistently for each home football game for several years.

Josh happened to be a junior during A&M's transition from the Big 12 to the SEC. Moreover, his Friday morning class schedule was purposefully light. As an engineering major Josh had plans each week as a one-man operation for lesser opponents and encouraged and facilitated the participation of more people for bigger games. In particular, he mentioned that for our first game against LSU, he was going to show up at 2:00 am to make sure our space was secured. I asked him if he was crazy? No one had ever shown up at that time. Sure 5:00 am, but not 2:00 am.

"Hey, we're *not* going to lose our great spot to some Tiger!" he answered.

Potluck

Little did we know how many years we would spend "winning" the tailgate, but losing the games to the team from Baton Rouge. Despite some occasional pre-SEC success with R.C. Slocum, it took a record-breaking performance in 2018 to secure a conference victory over the Tigers. Among other noteworthy accomplishments, that game set the record for the most combined points scored in a Division I FBS game, and the game had seven overtimes and lasted nearly five hours. The good guys, eventually, won 74-72.[19]

Now back to the story: I thought Josh was a great guy and how cool that Cheryl had taught him and worked with his father. The process of seeing people grow, develop, and mature into adults is amazing. We attended Josh's wedding, and while I can't tell you that Josh and his wife met at our tailgate, I will tell you that *we* met her at the tailgate. Lindsay is lovely, and we enjoyed spending time with her and others at the Varsity Tailgates.

Maybe there was something in the water of the key Varsity Tailgate contributors. Marty and Lauren were married after years of successfully managing the tailgate and are now expecting their first child. Chris and Lindsey—a different Lindsey—were married and he started his career with DuPont. See Chapter 2 - Surrounding Forces to learn more about his internship that helped to launch his career. Two other core contributors included Teddy and Cameron. Cameron recently married, and Teddy currently resides as the most eligible bachelor among the collegiate team that supports the Varsity

Tailgaters. We stay in touch and wish them all the best as their families and careers continue to grow. They made such a difference with their willingness to show up early and stay late over the years.

This team was on point because a big portion of tailgate execution and etiquette is making certain that you have a crew as good as ours, who is ready to unpack *all* the equipment immediately upon arrival. When you think about eight tents, 30 chairs, two TVs, two generators, and six or more tables, it becomes complicated quickly. If you show up and no one is there to help you unload, it can take hours. Done as a team in a coordinated fashion you can unpack in 15 minutes and be up and running in another 30 minutes. That's where the additional people listed earlier helped to make it happen. Notwithstanding the tailgate location and unpacking, you'll need someone to park the truck and trailer too.

Then after a *long* day of tailgating there's the breakdown, which is in and of itself a completely different adventure. Properly considered, a breakdown is somewhere between eight and 12 hours later and seemingly simply reverses the process established early. As you might expect, the breakdown is less precise than the setup.

The effects of "earth, wind, and fire" (see Chapter 3) are impactful. Not to mention the two w(h)e(a)thers (sic). Sure, there's the "weather" you might expect in the mud, the wind, and the sun that do impact the day. The other "whether" is whether or not your teams wins. Then, of course, whether or not someone consumed too much food or overindulged in beverages can also change things. Staying flexible and knowing that you will probably lose a few chairs, and maybe even a tent, at each tailgate is worth knowing and accepting up-front.

We often laugh that one of our key tailgaters is no longer allowed to break down tents because he would seemingly break one each week. Taking down the 10' x 10' tents requires the coordinated efforts of four people. Each person grabs a corner and walks toward the middle, while keeping an eye on how fast the others are moving as the metal connectors smartly collapse into a more condensed version of the tent for packing and storage. In that process, repeated close to a hundred times each season; if one person moves too fast, it throws off everyone else. Our friend would keep pushing, though, and one of the metal bars would eventually bend and crimp, if not break. The tents are rugged, but when this guy pushed too hard it was kink city, and pretty much game over for the future of that particular tent. He would get locked in on his section without keeping pace with the others. Pace, in a 12-hour day, especially at the end of the proverbial race, is important to everyone's success.

Cheryl's Thoughts

We quickly moved from small to big—from close family and friends to an extended group of students—and it got real. We now had to budget for everything. And we had to plan more to make sure everyone had food and drinks than anything else.

Know, too, that weather is a factor. Chili and cornbread when it's cold are perfect, and when it's hot, make sure you aren't putting out things that will spoil. My goal all along—which I think we succeeded at—had been to make sure that no one got sick.

Setting the expectation up-front with good communication is key. Proper planning makes the teamwork come together. In our family, grocery shopping was done on two separate days during the tailgating weeks.

Tuesday's groceries were for the family. Thursday's grocery shopping was for the tailgate. Then on Friday, I would come home and cook for the Saturday tailgates. Most people let me know what they were doing/bringing on Friday, and we had to work out the game plan. And 99% of the time, it really did work out well. When you hang around people like you, who are reliable, it's pretty cool. You get to see what everybody does when they come together as a team. It may sound silly, but teamwork does make the dream work.

While emails were a great communication tool before the game, on game day "text only" seemed to work better, which mattered to how we got things done. The group was very tech savvy, though, which also helped. With no Wi-Fi in the stadium and the overload of people onto the systems in College Station, it was likely that your phone would be dark for hours.

With texting as your only recourse on game days, the pre-planning efforts really came into focus. If you didn't plan, there were no last-minute heroes or people who could save the day—even if they or we wanted them to. Everything had to be set up beforehand in order to succeed.

What a great group of people. The generosity of the Varsity Tailgaters helped carry us through whatever the weather, the cell phone towers, or the Aggies brought to the stadium.

Beyond the Tailgate: Managing a successful tailgate requires a huge amount of communication, as well as reliable key contributors. The willingness to work through the issues by paying attention to the details is a key to success at your tailgate *and* in your relationships.

We thought we had it down, at times, even though we didn't. Everyone does want to contribute, and once you channel energy and provide direction, it helps. It's a bonding thing. Ask not what your tailgate can do for you, but what you can do for your tailgate—laugh out loud, if you will—but it's true.

CHAPTER 8

Managing the Messaging: Communication

Our View

As an advertising agency owner, I often discuss the concept of "marketing the marketing." At its core, marketing is about communication, and with all the platforms to do just that, there are ennumerable ways to convey what it is that you are trying to say.

One year I tested a group-texting app with our tailgating team that worked, but not well. Imagine several hundred texts lighting up around the campus, if not the state, simultaneously. It was good for outbound communication, but it sparked 100 inbound messages that could not be managed.

Our best platform turned out to be email well in advance of game day. We acknowledged where we were, what we were doing, when we were doing it, and how we needed to adjust moving forward.

We also acknowledged our sponsors. Take a look at this actual correspondence from an email blast before the Ole Miss tailgate in College Station during our tenth year of tailgating.

Varsity Tailgaters #10Yr Anniversary - BTHO Ole Miss

Howdy!

For the Rice University tailgate, we had 40 RSVPs and 120+ attendees. I heard feedback from sponsors, friends, and families, and we all agreed that we need your help to make a few adjustments as we move into SEC conference play.

Too many tailgate crashers @ this last go 'round!

To keep things manageable, we are going to go to PRIVATE tailgate status and limit to 100 guests. OUR guests. Wristbands only. Please make sure you RSVP. We love each and every one of you, but your RSVP is THE way to guarantee food, drink and ultimately participation as a Varsity Tailgater.

It's a new color wristband for Ole Miss!

It's out w/ the old and in w/ the new. Get your hands on one of the new wristbands. Please plan accordingly with your friends, family and coworkers since we have limited supplies and resources: food, drinks, funding, etc.

I appreciate your support in helping us to make and keep this a Varsity Tailgate!

The Ole Miss Varsity Tailgate will be up and running @ 2:00 pm with food from Kilburn's Tavern and the Cowboy Mardi Gras Cook Team. We will start with wings around 3:30 pm and will roll out the rest between then and 5:30 pm. Plans include brisket, chopped beef sandwiches, smoked jalapeno cheddar sausage, baked beans, Cajun mashed potatoes. and some vegetable dishes as well. Thanks again John Burr and John Montgomery!

My sister—an Ole Miss graduate—and her family will be at the tailgate and game. My dad—who'll be wearing maroon—will be there as well. I hope y'all get to meet them and say Howdy!

The game kicks off @ 8:00 p.m. It'll be a nice night to BTHO outta Ole Miss!

Gig 'em Aggies,

Jim and Cheryl Flint '94

Separately, this email served to highlight our sponsors:

We spend hundreds of hours and thousands of dollars supporting our tailgating habit. Please support our sponsors as well as our friends and families when and where you can. Local Search Group Digital Marketing will be providing 10th Anniversary wristbands. Hold on to these. We want to make sure the tailgate REMAINS family and friends and this will be one of the keys.

Karbach is a top-flight Texas microbrew company. Actually, one of the best brewers in a smoking hot category. I mean you aren't the one bringing a six pack of Bud Light to the holiday party, right? So, check out Weisse Versa, Hopadillo, or Weekend Warrior on Saturday. Twenty-one and older only, please. Jake, thanks for your local support and to Blake and Adam for all their efforts.

Cowboy Mardi Gras Cookers will be serving up their award-winning food for the first three home games this year! If you don't catch them here you can see them @ the Houston Rodeo and spots throughout Texas during the fall.

Pepper - Lawson joins the Varsity Tailgating Crew for an encore engagement. As one of the top construction companies in town and with some of the best people in the business, they are a welcome addition and great supporter. Thanks to Chad and Jenn.

(If anyone for any reason would like to be removed from this email list, please send a reply email to me, and I will take care of for you with no questions asked.)
As mentioned earlier, my sister went to Ole Miss. Our nephew, Flint, now attends school in Oxford, Mississippi, and Philip does

as well. Tailgates in Oxford are substantially different than those in College Station. First and foremost, College Station, comparatively, has wide open spaces. You can spread out and stretch your legs a bit. In Oxford, you are jam-packed in the Grove. We've been to at least three tailgates in the Grove to see the Aggies play Ole Miss. As mentioned throughout, family runs strong. We love my sister and brother-in-law (University of Southern Mississippi), but I couldn't help but capture the sentiments of Ole Miss when I chose to publish this blog on TailgatingIdeas.com in 2010.[20]

Ole Miss Chooses Academics Over Tailgating

In a move that surprised many, Ole Miss decided to choose academics over tailgating. Separately and possibly equally as surprising, the university decided to keep tailgating free of charge.

How many Rebels does it take to make these kind of tough decisions? Turns out a 60-person committee came up with the new proposal that now prohibits tailgate setups of any kind prior to 10:00 pm on Friday night. Apparently, too many students were missing classes on Friday to help set up tailgates at the Grove. Some overachievers in Oxford may have missed classes on Wednesday and Thursday too—when one considers the size of the Rebel tailgate nation.

In discussing the new policy, Ole Miss wrote that they '... want to preserve [the] campus for its core mission of academics.'

We had a good laugh about the pronouncement.

Our family has been to no less than four A&M vs. Ole Miss games—three in Oxford and one in College Station. Each time the road team walked away from the game victorious. The best story, though, likely comes from our first tailgate in Oxford.

A&M had just joined the SEC, and everyone was looking forward to the trip to Oxford and tailgating in the Grove. A few weeks out, we found out that we would be buoyed by a 6:00 pm. kickoff time. There were some obstacles to overcome, however. First up, the Aggie Nation travels well. No hotel rooms were available in Oxford, so we had to book rooms in Batesville, Mississippi which is 23.5 miles from Vaught-Hemingway stadium. Moreover, during the day a drizzly, chilly cold front moved through the campus and settled over us. The temperature had dropped into the mid-30s by early evening.

My dad, who was up from Biloxi, and one of our friends, Steve, who made the trip up from Houston, utilized some adult beverages to help keep themselves warm. My dad--repeatedly, throughout the day--advised that he would be leaving the game at halftime so he could make it back to New Orleans to see his beloved Saints play a game against the San Diego Chargers the next day. To his credit, Oxford is about nine hours away from New Orleans, and he only planned to make it halfway home from Oxford to Jackson, Mississippi on Saturday night. Logistical, contextual explanations aside: he would not be there after the game.

As we broke from the day of chilly, wet tailgating on our path to the stadium we separated into groups. My nephews, brother-in-law and I went to the car to get some rain gear and try to warm up before further immersion into the inhospitable weather conditions. Cheryl and my sister went a different route, and Steve and my dad went off in their own direction. We all had our own tickets in hand in Section 105, the visitor's section, and had agreed to meet there. As it turned out, on the way into the stadium, my Dad and Steve ran into some friendly types, who had also been keeping warm during the icy-cold day via their friend, Jack Daniels. The locals had 50-yard line tickets for sale. The out-of-towners had cash in hand.

"Just $20 for each ticket," said one of the locals, who for all intents and purposes had decided to stay out of the rain and freezing cold.

"I'll give you $20 for both," said my dad. The two locals from Oxford shared one knowing glance and the deal was done. The locals were going to watch the game at the comfort of their tailgate or more than likely by the fireplace in their own homes.

Bolstered by their spirit and their spirits my dad and Steve forged ahead down a new path to a different part of the stadium--pretty much on the 50-yard line. The remainder of the group re-connected as we found our places in our very satisfactory end zone seats. We bought some hot chocolate and attempted to stay warm as we made the best of a bad weather situation.

At the end of the first quarter we received a text from our

"missing" revelers. Steve and dad advised us of their good fortune. Their new seats were great!

At the end of the second quarter, my Dad texted again to let us know that he was, as previously mentioned and often discussed, indeed leaving at halftime. He noted in his text: "You might want to check on Steve."

We enjoyed the half-time shows. The Ole Miss band and the Aggie band each performed admirably in the artic elements. It was so cold, and the rain persisted. Icy, frosty rain. We were wet. Our shoes were soaked. An uncomfortable chill was settling into our feet. We'd been tailgating since lunchtime, and it was now past 10:00 pm.

To provide perspective, Flint and Philip were twelve and ten years old, respectively at the time, and they were quite understandably ready to leave. Who cared about the score? Age notwithstanding, the adults were ready to go, too. We no longer felt our fingers, toes, or even our noses. It was the beginning of the third quarter, and we had a 30-minute drive back to our hotel—without mentioning the necessity of finding two separate cars in the sleety precipitation after a full day of tailgating.

Pageantry of the bands adequately accomplished, we wanted to beat the traffic and head back to Batesville ahead of the crowd. Surprisingly, given the weather conditions, the crowd was pretty decent well into the third quarter. Not surprisingly and, like most schools in the SEC, Oxford is not designed to have so many people departing from the game at the same time. My sister advised that traffic jams would easily take us well past midnight.

We were ready to go and Steve would be arriving any moment. He had just texted as such.

With Dad long gone, the remainder of the team had assembled near one of the stadium exits and secured one last check to see if anyone objected to the early departure. We were good...except there was no Steve. We checked again. We texted. There was a long delay. Maybe the cell towers in Oxford were just as bad as the ones in College Station?

Then out of nowhere he texted, "I'll get a taxi back."

This was not the age of Uber, and there were no taxis in Oxford. He would have had the equivalent hike of a marathon in suboptimal weather conditions as the chill now settled heavier into the night.

Someone in our group of six asked if we should go, and Cheryl famously pronounced, "No man left behind."

See the following map to know that Steve was standing in Section J as we waited just outside of Gate 106.

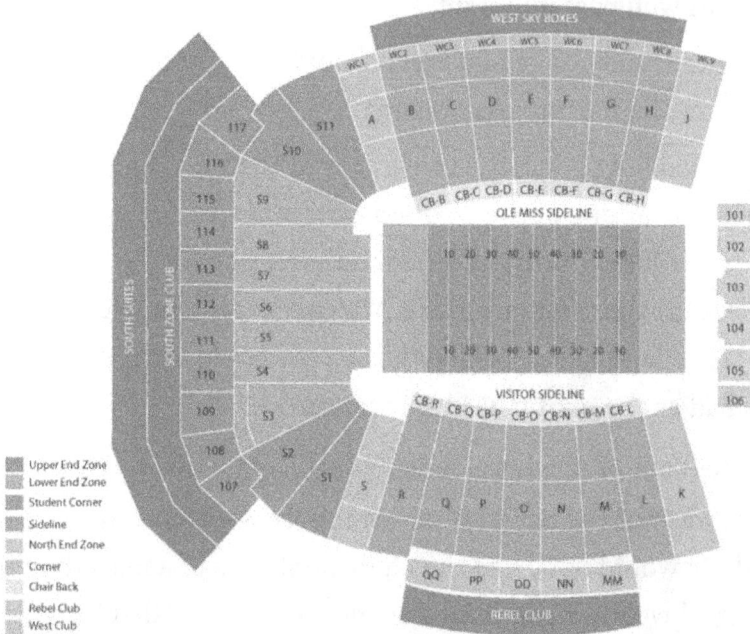

Upper End Zone
Lower End Zone
Student Corner
Sideline
North End Zone
Corner
Chair Back
Rebel Club
West Club

When the text responses become fewer and further between, I tried calling Steve, and by the grace of God the call went through and he picked up. It was now midway through the third quarter, and he was incoherently describing how the ticket taker would *not* let him out of Section J, even though he had a ticket. His original ticket—which was still unused—would not work because you can't leave and reenter an SEC stadium per conference rules. Our friend was, you could tell, exasperated. I told him to tell me where he was in the Ole Miss Stadium.

"SECTION J!," he bellowed.

I leapt into action and kept Steve on the phone. As I moved from Section 106 to Section J, Steve continued to ramble on the phone. There was a ticket taker that would keep me from going through Section 101 through to Section J though.

Steve was ranting and raving: " I just cannot believe..."

I held up the phone and told the ticket taker, "Look, my friend needs to be saved, and he's in Section J!" I was now underneath Section 101. Arguably, a long, hail-mary pass would have connected us.

However, the ticket taker politely advised: "You will need to walk around the stadium to connect with him."

"I'm thinking he's going to get into trouble, and we just want to take him home," I said.

"I'd have to let you down onto the field, and I can't do that," she said.

Steve was ranting and raving in the background as I held the phone up and placed the call on speaker for her to listen. He was rambling incoherently.

"What if I walked right down and right back up to keep your whole security team from having to deal with this typically mild-mannered guy?" I continued, "What if you looked right over there, and I walked right down there and by the time you looked back I was gone."

She looked left. I moved swiftly right.

Without hesitation, I walked down to the field, grazed the pylon in the end zone, and smartly jumped over the rail into Section J. A play was being executed on the other end of the field. I marched up the steps to find our friend. For a microsecond Steve's expression was relief. He was glad to see me; however, that microsecond later, his rant had acquired new vigor, "How'd you get in here? This place is insane. I can't believe they let you in. They sure wouldn't let me out. Or at least back in. This place is insane. And we're losing to Ole Miss. We're going to lose to Ole Miss. Insanity I tell you."

The redundancy in his words wasn't lost on me, but I had our man; we made it back to our core group and were headed back with Steve in tow. No man had been left behind. A brisk fifteen minute walk later and we were in our cars and on our way to Batesville. Certainly warmer, the group had begun drying out and were feeling much toastier and happier than when we'd originally left.

A year later, my nephews gave Steve copies of the game program and storyboards to commemorate the occasion of the "No Man Left Behind Tailgate."

This was a pregame gift to him before the second of the Aggies back-to-back games in Oxford in 2013. It was another night game, and it was chilly, but nowhere near what it had been the year before. We again secured tickets in the end zone. This time Steve stayed close.

In the aforementioned first Oxford game, Johnny Manziel directed a dramatic comeback that helped to establish himself as a worthy Heisman candidate—an award he secured during his as well as the Aggies first season in the SEC. In his second game in Oxford, Johnny Football led another exciting comeback and a different family-based story line developed.

We continue to re-tell it through the years. In the 2013 edition, Ole Miss and Texas A&M completed a closely contested battle that had everyone on the edge of their seats. As the clock ticked down, Josh Lambo's 33-yard Aggie field goal sailed through the uprights to help Texas A&M win the game as time expired.[21] My eleven-year old nephew was wearing an Ole Miss T-shirt and had been sitting in the Aggie section. His mom, my sister and a graduate of Ole Miss, and he wanted their team to win the game. He became upset at about the same time that the field goal kick hit the protective net somewhere close to 20 yards away from our seats.

As we were walking out, an unknown adult Aggie started making made fun of him for taking the tough loss so hard. Aunt Cheryl stepped in with, "Aggies don't lie, cheat, or steal, and they certainly don't make fun of children."

She had used the Aggie code of honor to admonish an older gentleman for picking on a child. The older man received a similar rebuke from what appeared to be his significant other, if not his wife.

"Sorry, kid. Better luck next year," he said for all to hear in a self-correcting manner.

A year later in 2014, Ole Miss did have better short-term luck. As detailed in the email earlier in this chapter, we welcomed my family and over 110,630 people into Kyle Field to watch the #3 ranked Rebels play the #14 Aggies. The attendance level set the all-time-attendance record for Kyle Field.[22] Despite the on the field victory, the Ole Miss football team later vacated wins from 33 games, including this one, as part of the results of an NCAA investigation.[23]

Cheryl's Thoughts

You really do have to communicate the plan more than once to the group. Remind. Recap. And as an educator, I could get frustrated because I spend so much time during my week doing exactly this. Are there any educators out there who can relate? But it's really necessary.

If people can't find you when it matters, and when people can't talk to you, it's tough. We've gotten better about giving more details and making adjustments to make it work for more people. The bigger your family gets, the better it gets, but that requires even more communication as you go.

We were trying to reach different people at different times and on their wavelengths. The overwhelming majority of tailgaters did not come from College Station, so we were talking to people from all over the state, if not region.

I get credit for the "No Man Left Behind" game, and I'm glad it was an away game to help over emphasize the importance of the message. In general, you don't forget about people, no matter where you may be. If someone comes to a game to tailgate with you and can't find you, for any reason, it misses the point of having a tailgating community. Sometimes you have to go find people and bring them back. In the moment it's good to know your group's core principles. Tailgating is not the Marines nor the military for that matter, but it mattered, though, for what it meant to my family and what my nephews took away from the experience as well.

The following year "Protect Your Family" just happened in the moment because I couldn't have adults—from the college I went to—messing with my sweetie pie nephews. It's ironic to hear the story from my nephew's, Flint Christian, viewpoint Yes, his first name is our surname. Give my sister-in-law Cindy and brother-in-law Andrew credit for that. At any rate, Flint said I came across *strong* in my communication to my fellow Ag. Again, the educator in me came out. I did not want my nephews to be turned off for a lifetime because some Aggies were winning in the Southeastern Conference and did not quite know how to handle themselves. Being gracious is a learned skilled. I just didn't want to be as rude to the Aggie fans as they were being to my nephew.

To their credit, the Good Ag did step up and apologize. And that's the thing about Aggies: we adjust and have become much more gracious winners than many others in our state. I can't wait to be gracious one day—during my lifetime—when we win the National Championship. One day I tell you! I care more about that than the Super Bowl. I'm really not trying to brag, but for various reasons I've been to some Super Bowls and really can't wait to feel the excitement of having the Aggies play in and someday winning the big game at the NCAA level.

I prefer college sports and feel that they are more attractive, albeit admittedly less polished. The NFL is so polished. I love the idea of what could be, and to watch the development of the players actually happen is so incredible. The grit athletes display on a daily basis represents what you have to do to take care of your family, your business community and yourself. Watching college athletes develop into NFL players is amazing. I prefer college to the NFL and seeing the growth the players go through is probably why.

Beyond the Tailgate: Family matters, and you do have to look out for, if not protect your family of friends, players, and work associates. Communicate with everyone, and then communicate some more. Communication is the first thing to go in a relationship. Be willing to talk about what's happening and, at the same time, be willing to adjust to any given situation. The "No Man Left Behind" and the "Protect Your Family" principles are solid core philosophies for tailgating or otherwise.

CHAPTER 9

Beyond the Bandwagon:
Reputation Matters

Our View

*E*very tailgate weekend takes on its own nuances, but the tailgate culture lives on from week-to-week and year-to-year. What happens at the tailgate lives on forever in the way of stories—via books like this one and the legacies of great tailgaters like Joe Cahn, the founder of the New Orleans School of Cooking and self-proclaimed "commissioner of tailgating." When you combine all the elements properly, the atmosphere is charged with energy. Emotions arrive with big crowds and with the hope of a victory each week and the promising rebirth of each and every season.

One of greatest rebirths in the history of sport happened when the Aggies joined the Southeastern Conference in 2012. The second largest Varsity Tailgate in our history happened during that season opener versus the University of Florida. We had a new football coach in Kevin Sumlin and a new quarterback that many referred to as Johnny Football.

The Aggies opening home game—also the SEC conference opener—in the inaugural season in the conference was against legendary SEC university and former national champion Florida. The Aggies introduction to the new league was a dream matchup. The enthusiasm was incredible, and the move to the conference had been positioned as a 100-year decision by university administration.[24] The Aggies were moving out from under the shadow of their in-state brethren.

As the weekend approached, almost everyone eagerly anticipated this over the top onboarding moment that would mark history. The rookies, the veterans and everyone in between wanted to go to the tailgate, if not the game. As kickoff approached, we learned that Jägermeister had donated a chilled dispenser to our tailgate. We remember looking at the contraption with such awe when we hooked it up to the generator. When the machine came to life, a blue LED light delivered the message that the contents within the machine had been chilled to 8°. Meanwhile, it was closer to 95° outside the tailgate tents in the nearby September sun. Many of our tailgaters advised me that the drink felt like 8°. Experienced tailgaters know not to work at the extremes of any equation, much less ones like this; however, some of our veteran tailgaters were just much too caught up in the SEC moment. One person, who went too far too fast ,was encouraged to "chill" for a bit in his truck. He ended up sleeping away the rest of the Aggies' SEC opening afternoon. This story lives on with him. For the good and the bad of it, it is his to own and somewhat surprisingly he does so fondly with just a bit of chagrin and a shrug of his shoulders for having missed the entirety of the game.

A couple with no relationship to our tailgating crew engaged in quite a bit of public display of affection right outside of our tent. The sun was setting on a beautiful day, and they too were arguably caught up in the moment. With cameras and phones everywhere, people started taking pictures and videos. Our sponsors' logos were in the background, so I walked over to the couple, somehow interrupted them, and asked them in a friendly way to find another place to celebrate the day.

This couple may or may not have realized that social media is everywhere. We did not register our tailgate on Google Places—although we could have—and we pretty much stayed away from Facebook until the very end, but today we would guide younger tailgaters just getting started that digital images—video and pictures—will live on forever. More on that in Chapter 11- Social Media Patterns.

As part of reputation development on the positive side of the ledger, we wanted to develop positive shared histories with our friends, families, and people passing by. On many weekends we gave away T-shirts and koozies from our sponsors. They were good marketing materials.

It also helps to think about your reputation as it relates to your family and your coworkers. We were conscious of encouraging a family-friendly atmosphere. At the same time, though, most tailgates are *not* for teetotalers. We wanted to make sure that people had a great time. "All good things in moderation" is a great tagline and a good way to approach any event, much less a twelve-hour tailgating marathon. For what it's worth sprinters don't typically fare all that well at tailgates.

Another thing you can do to enhance or even protect your reputation as a tailgater is to introduce yourself to the people you do not know. Due to our popular location, this not only happened quite a bit, it became an important way to ensure that tailgate crashing did not reach epidemic proportions.

One way to think about it is that no one is a stranger at the tailgate! We would extend a hand, introduce ourselves, and welcome someone to our tailgate with a "Howdy!" We would then quickly ask who the person knew from the tailgate so we could connect the dots and introduce them around.

We learned this concept from the San Antonio Spurs head coach Gregg Popovich during high school. At the time, Popovich was an assistant coach with the Spurs, and the team often practiced at Incarnate Word College in San Antonio.[25] Cheryl, her brothers, and one of our good friends, Trent May, would go to Spurs practice when we were in high school. Trent played college ball and followed up with a successful career coaching college basketball.[26] We all spoke the love language of sports, if not Spurs, and the Spurs were the only big-time sports game in town. These were the lottery-pick Spurs before David Robinson, Tim Duncan, Manu Ginobili, and what, ultimately, turned into five championship rings.

One January morning the winds were particularly blustery, so we decided to wait in the hallway just outside the practice gymnasium. We could see the scrimmage just getting started.

As we shivered and warmed ourselves, Coach Pop walked toward us with his head down. When he finally reached us, he looked up and in a way that only he could have and asked us, "Hey do you guys know any of the players?" The five of us— none of us who had graduated from college--looked at each other and then back at the coach and said, "No, sir."

Coach Pop shook his head empathetically and with his own seemingly personal reminder that he had a job to do he followed with, "Hey I know it's cold outside, and it's nothing against you, but if you don't know any of the players on the team, you can't wait in here."

It was polite. It was professional. And it acknowledged the obvious. If we did not have a connection with one of the players, we could not stay. A decade later, we utilized the same principles with our tailgate.

Marty Mulgrew was one of the best at the tailgate with this particular responsibility. He served, like Popovich, as an able assistant by ensuring that the tailgate stayed "players only." Plus, he liked meeting and introducing people and connecting them when they knew someone in our tailgate. The beauty of the Popovich approach is that it acknowledges the person *and* it, importantly, acknowledges that they may be connected to someone who is part of the team. If they are not part of the family and therefore should not be there, it allows them to politely recognize the situation and opt out on their own.

Many times, there would be a connection to the tailgate, and we could easily bring the people together; however, about 5% of the time people were waiting for the crosswalk to clear before walking over to the stadium and just wanted to check things out. For those people, we provided koozies mostly or T-shirts from the sponsors when the situation called for it.

Friendliness Translates. A Howdy! A Handshake! A Gift!

It's amazing what happens when twelve or more core people, our tailgate team, start connecting with various tailgaters or people who turn out to be connected to others throughout a day, a season, and the years. We quickly earned a "friendly" reputation. We considered it a good way to serve as an international host for all the visiting schools that would come through as well. We wanted to make sure everyone had a great time, and we had connections to the thousands of people who happened by our tailgate.

With so much traffic walking by our location each weekend, things did become hectic. As game time came closer, traffic officers directed cars and people. As cars flowed, the waiting people would stand adjacent to our tailgate. While waiting for their turn to cross the street and head into the stadium, we were happy to have people take promotional items.

The reputation you have also influences the sponsorships you can acquire. The reputation we secured at the end of the day was also family-friendly fun and that should make sense for most of the people reading this book. Either way, though, think about your goals in this regard because it will attract the right kinds of people to your tailgate as it continues to grow. It also attracts different sponsors. Chapter 10 goes into tailgating and the sponsorship process in greater depth. Even if you don't have a family of tailgaters yet, you will, and as you think back to

Chapter 2 - Surrounding Forces, remember that you will become the average of the five people you spend the most time with in your lives. Consider that carefully as you think about the reputation you will be building.

Traditions Matter Too

Reputation matters with regard to how you handle the traditions of your tailgate and the teams you support. One of the many great traditions at A&M is to "dunk" your class ring. The 1970s tradition started in the Dixie Chicken when a Corps of Cadets member accidentally dropped his ring in the bottom of a pitcher of beer and drank the pitcher in order to get his ring back. We have several tailgaters from our crew and some surrounding crews who conducted the ceremony at our tailgate each year.

Our evolution of reputation occurred over time and so, too, will yours.

We initially became known as the "technology tailgaters" and then evolved to the "blogging tailgaters." We were also called "friendly" tailgaters mostly. Only later ,when we integrated these three facets with an improved food factor, did we earn our "Varsity Tailgating" status. We even had a license plate for the trailer: "VRSTY" with SEC stickers on it.

Just as importantly the Varsity Tailgate name had a story behind it that infused, galvanized and substantiated our culture.

We wanted to do things at a higher level which helped our team as we shared the story with others. It was a challenging standard to live up to, but one that our tailgating team chose to embrace.

At some point we recognized that our tailgate was a brand, as well. To extend our reputation we created a logo and placed it on every item we imagine. We put our logos on platters, tablecloths, plates, koozies, and tents. In the end, you could find our logo almost anywhere.

You should think of your tailgate and, at some level, your relationships and family as brands with logos, too.

In the magical tenth year—ten years is a long time for relationships, tailgates, or almost anything—we purchased Varsity Tailgater collared polos for our key tailgaters. Sure, we had T-shirts, but we wanted to have something extra special as we continued to do things at a higher level.

Scholarship Fund

In 2018 we were proud, yet humbly able, to create the next chapter of stories that will exist for others beyond Aggie tail-gates by way of the Cheryl and Jim Flint '94 Scholarship. We did this through Cheryl's college, the Biomedical and Veterinarian School of Medicine. Thank you to Chastity Carrigan '16, assistant vice president for development at Texas A&M, for showing us the way.[27] She established her own endowed scholarship while working for the school at the same time she was earning her master's degree. Talk about an overachiever! When we met her, she helped us fall more in love with the university. Through Chastity, we were able to meet our first scholarship student—appropriately enough at the Vet School tailgate—just before the Clemson vs. Texas A&M game in Kyle Field in 2018.

Cheryl's Thoughts

I wasn't trying to leave a legacy; I just wanted to connect with people. It all happened from humble beginnings. The tailgate grew into a monster, but it was a gentle giant. People were getting what they needed from the experience. The word "legacy" can sound vain so I shy away from it; the "reputation" of the tailgate was a real byproduct of what was otherwise just wanting to spend more time with family and friends that spoke the love language of sports.

I suppose the reputation builds as you go, but what I know is that the people we were with did what they said they would do. And if that happens to be our reputation--that we had a fun tailgate while bringing people together—that's really what it all came down to.

No matter how exhausted I was after a tailgating weekend, getting the thank you emails and texts on Monday afternoon meant so much to me. More often than not, less than 48 hours removed from the previous tailgate, people were already looking forward to the next one!

Beyond the Tailgate: Reputation matters. It's not what you should aim for though. Day-to-day thinking, overall consistency, the culture you create, and who you surround yourself with on a daily basis will be what ultimately determines what you're know for in the long run. That's how reputations grow—one tailgate, one person, one family member at a time.

Chapter 10

﮼

Getting Sponsored

"Sponsorship can come to you in different ways. You never know who is watching you, so be 'sponsor-ready' at all times."

—*Millette Granville, author of The Exceptional Leader*

Our View

As you look out on the tailgate landscape, you'll recognize that football is the country's most popular sport. In-stadium sponsorships can be expensive and may only reach 80,000 to 100,000 fans. Outside the stadium, you may reach an equal number of excited, passionate fans with more time to engage with a product.[28]

After several years of work and ample amounts of sweat equity, we realized we needed additional financial contributors *and* we would need to secure sponsors to keep up with everything we had going on with the tailgate. Although many of our key contributors were college juniors or seniors, we had one tailgater who owned and operated three successful businesses of his own, John Burr provided excellent guidance, a love for sports, and overall alignment with the culture we were creating.

As we were making our sponsorship presentations, Texas A&M was very much involved in conference realignment. Before the Aggies made the jump to the SEC, there were rumors and speculation about major changes. Would they go to the PAC-12? What would happen with Nebraska leaving the Big 12 for the Big 10. Would TCU or the University of Houston be invited to the Big 12? A&M would never leave Texas, right?

For almost two consecutive years the conversations ebbed, flowed and decidedly peaked during the summer months. Sports talk radio had found refuge from the doldrums of summer sports as college football's conference realignment possibilities dominated the airwaves. On August 31, 2012, A&M announced that they would leave the Big 12 and join the SEC. Missouri would be joining, too and the conference would grow to 14 teams.

At this point, we also had been in *the* top tailgating location for years. Several forces Beyond the Tailgate had worked together to drive our thinking to the next level:

- We were tapped out financially.
- We were on the geographical front line with high visibility.
- The Aggies were going to the next level, and we, culturally, had been about moving things to the next level.
- Sponsorships could be more effective and less costly.

The realignment of collegiate conferences created buzz, and we had the inside track to one of the biggest conversations in Texas. Former Texas A&M president James Loftin referenced the move to the SEC as a 100-year decision.[29]

And that's what we let potential sponsors know. The presentation included Google Map elements to identify our location and, having worked on sponsorships for Nike and Toyota in my professional life, we were able to generate presentations that worked. We convinced, we compelled, and we worked to connect with the possibility of what it all could and, ultimately, would become.

In reviewing the presentations for purposes of the book, the nostalgia flowed back as our support plans revealed itself to me retroactively. During the presentations, we highlighted the following:

- Active tailgaters since 2005;
- A 23-14 record on the field – *undefeated* at the tailgate;
- A national tailgating blog: TailgatingIdeas.com with 50,000 visitors a month and a lead writer;
- Tailgating passion and presence—with tens of thousands of sports-minded enthusiasts walking by each week;
- A preseason Top Ten team; and
- An all-new conference and the country's best conference to boot—the Southeastern Conference.

We added pictures of our tailgating crew to humanize our team. Google Maps helped show how close we were to Kyle Field, and we highlighted the growth that was occurring in terms of sponsorships in their competitive categories vis-a-vis nearby, competitive tailgating sponsorships. We found that our sponsors became significantly more engaged when they saw that some-one from within their product space had established a presence with consumers that had a passion for college football.

We had a ton of energy, excitement, and enthusiasm, but just like in your relationships, it helps to have a steadying influence. John Burr proved to be just that. There were no less than half a dozen preliminary presentations that were reviewed and presented before we were ready to meet with the factory representatives. Several distributors, beer sponsors, food sponsors, car dealerships, construction companies, and even a fishing rod and reel company were in the potential sponsor mix. We nailed down the presentations and, more often than not, the sponsorships as well. Like many former students of Texas A&M, John was an electrical engineer, and although not a former student he did provide important behind the scenes support. He was willing to make trades with his suppliers in order to help his companies, their companies, and our tailgate. As a member of the Mardi Gras Cook team, he also helped facilitate that connection and often went above and beyond to supply just the right amount of food at countless tailgates.

Another key player in the evolution of our tailgate was Mac DeLaup. He had an interesting request off the bat. He wanted to bring the young tailgaters in for a meeting to hear their perspectives on what the tailgate could be each year. What a great way to galvanize the troops and for the sponsor(s) to hear what was going on with the millennial generation. Moreover, key influencers would learn more about his dealership. He included the logos for his companies on koozies, tents, t-shirts and the like.

As a family, we also talked about what the dynamic of adding sponsorships meant to us. One of our key conversations centered on the baseline belief that the sponsorships would help us to keep things family, friendly, and fun on a go-forward basis. As mentioned in Chapter 9--Reputation Matters, we were now escalating our commitments. Not only were we willing to look out for our own reputations, but we were willing and able to look out for our sponsors' reputations as well. As it turns out, you can often do things more effectively for others than you might otherwise be able to do just for yourself. Point being, we were looking out for the greater good in an even bigger way.

Another focal point involved when sponsors visited our tailgate. We made sure that all the items they had provided us were proudly displayed every week; however, when they visited we tried to determine the best ways to take their sponsorships to the next level. One advancement was that even though our sponsors were included on the weekly emails—even if they were not attending—we smartly evolved to a place that highlighted a different "sponsor of the week" at the beginning of the weekly emails. Additionally, after the conclusion of games, we emailed pictures of the event to the sponsors so they knew they were getting exactly what they had bargained for, if not more.

Throughout the season, the emails proved to be highly effective, and we were sure to follow-up with personal invitations for the sponsors to join us.

We also encouraged the sponsors to share our emails with their employees and asked them to let us know when anyone from their teams would be joining us. They were all invited; they just needed to communicate timing with us.

Remember the mention of earning a reputation as a "friendly" tailgate? We made sure to welcome our sponsors with equal, if not greater, enthusiasm. We tried to find tickets for sponsors, too, when and if it made sense. If they had children, we encouraged them to bring them along—especially if they were students at the university. We were honest, fair, and took responsibility for keeping our promises to our sponsors. The sponsors treated us well, and we, in turn, treated them well. Their support provided us with all the right things at all the right times in order to take our Varsity Tailgates to the next level.

Cheryl's Thoughts

The right support makes all the difference because sometimes the wrong support, or lack of support altogether, doesn't get you to the goal. There needs to be a common thread of the same purpose among team members. Sometimes goals can be different, and knowing that up front is important. Whether that's overall goals or even from tailgate to tailgate.

Dry ice is one good example. One person offered up dry ice

to our tailgate. What we needed for hot September games were huge fans (not people, but industrial grade fans to help circulate the air in and around the tailgate area. Our sponsors came through.

Being comfortable in your environment is critical for the attendees, and the sponsors helped us with that goal. Another thing people like to do is take away mementos or souvenirs of the day, so our wristbands, T-shirts, and koozies served that purpose for our tailgaters, as well as our sponsors.

Being sponsored also means being supported...from sources both seen and unseen. Some of our sponsors helped us to see the blind spots, if you will. Different insights from the different types of sponsors helped us gain a better perspective. With their help we were able to see the gaps and fill them.

Sometimes Jim will do something or make a plan and I ask if we really need it, but then it hits me that was a sponsor's idea that I didn't even recognize we needed, but was always a great idea. In that process, I became rejuvenated many times.

There has to be faith in the human condition for all of humanity. I found this on ourselves and others--especially sponsors.

The people who helped us reach more people were part of the sponsorship, too. The college students who gave time, energy, and love were sponsors in more of a physical and emotional sense, which cannot be underestimated.

Reaching the next level on anything takes a village to get it right. You could be an island, I suppose, but that does not seem like it would be as much fun or nearly as interesting.

You cannot help but feel gratitude toward sponsors, and

while they did not always come to the games, you want to reciprocate. Especially if you are a people pleaser. Over the years I was amazed by the time, energy, emotional and financial commitment people made in contributing to something bigger themselves.

The whole point was the goal: spending quality time together and creating positive shared histories. Regardless of the score of the game, people had a really incredible time. This fall, one of my friends posted a picture on their Facebook page from a tailgate with the message: "I sure miss our tailgates!". Stay tuned for more on social media in the next chapter.

Beyond the Tailgate: You need support to get where you are going in life. Having the right structure will make things better for you, your family, and all those around you. I think everyone wants to be and likes being part of something bigger than themselves. That's what family means to begin with, right?

CHAPTER 11

Training Days and Social Media Patterns

"Privacy is dead and social media holds the smoking gun."

-Pete Cashmere, Founder of mashable.com

Our View

One of our most promising young tailgaters was Sarah. She enjoyed the competition, was a former A&M student, and, much like Cheryl, she enjoyed the ride to and from College Station a great deal. Each year, in our efforts to continuously improve, we had a "Training Day" get together at our house before the seasons started. Sure, we wanted to have a good time, but there were new people like Sarah who could and wanted to contribute more to the tailgate than they had the year before.

Given all the prework that goes into a successful tailgating season, we brought Sarah on board via the aforementioned training day. In so doing it started to crystalize that one day of training isn't that much to trade for a lifetime of fun. Tailgates involve trading time and preparation for future positive experiences. So what does a training day look like?

Tailgaters' Training Day

Since tailgating training happens in the "off-season," it's all about the upcoming season and what you can do to take your tailgating and your team to the next level. A few thought starters...to get your juices flowing as you look to start fresh just before the beginning of football season.

Look at the calendar—for example, is Halloween on a Saturday this year? Huge for home games that day.

Get your equipment right. If you haven't done so already, test your generator and do all the required maintenance. Don't leave gasoline in the generator all winter, spring, and summer and expect your unit to work like a charm in the fall. Toss in a packet of fuel stabilizer, crank it up, and you should be good to go.

Upgrade your equipment. A generator makes the single biggest difference in taking your tailgate to the next level. The first three years we didn't have one, and we were limited. Now with just 2,000 watts, we have so many options that it's ridiculous.

If you already have a generator, don't be the guy with one of the industrial generators that makes the kind of noise typically reserved for a construction site. Do everyone a favor and purchase a new generator this year if you are "that guy." You know the kind, just downwind, with the generator that puts out

10,000 watts and seemingly delivers just about as many decibels of noise. Not to mention the gas fumes. Unbearable for everyone. If you have anything but a Honda generator, think about buying one. After exhaustive research, the A2000 is the best of the bunch for price, reliability, noise, and performance.

Watch *Training Day* with an Academy-Award-winning performance from Denzel Washington. Then go to former student get togethers and speak with recent graduates about catching up with you and your crew at the tailgate. Potential protégés will bring lots of energy and fun to the table. Tell them, though, that before they attend a tailgate they should watch the movie, too. After watching—if they get "it"—you've got the right people coming to your tailgate. If they don't get "it," don't try to explain; it's already too late. Part of the deal is recognizing that tailgating, while certainly a performance sport, is a marathon and not a sprint. With that knowledge they will be well served. If not, the trainees first few trips will make for interesting times at your tailgate. "Too much, too soon" can be equally entertaining albeit potentially disappointing.

Planning for a Real Training Day

A good tailgate doesn't come off cleanly without some great teamwork. Taking the time to ensure the TVs work and that your tables aren't on their last legs is highly recommended. There's nothing worse than getting to that first tailgate and finding out that you only have three usable chairs, a remote control without batteries, and an empty fuel tank for the grill.

Stretch the Thinking

Jim bring up a few outlandish ideas that aren't likely to be achieved each year during the off-season. Whether or not the concept can be achieved doesn't really matter. What does matter is that it helps make the more reasonable requests seem to be just that: more reasonable. While you may not get the Jacuzzi you want for the tailgate, you will be able to get buy-in on the hi-def satellite TV package you're looking to land.

His lead item one year was a big yellow school bus for tailgate transport. The buses run $3k to $7k, and while tit never happened. It did help to keep other dreams alive.[30]

Let's Talk Social Media Pros and Cons

Social media is intertwined in our lives and with your tailgate. Our initial foray into tailgating proved to have fortuitous timing in that—especially so early on--we did not have the issue of people publishing to TikTok, Facebook, Snapchat, Instagram, Twitter, or the like. Call it what you will, but as we progressed, it became more important to have a plan for social media as well as your attendees' phones.

By way of Snapchat's introduction of the "stories" concept and the corresponding effective adjustments by Instagram and Facebook as well as launches by upstarts like TikTok, social media continues to thrive. Rest assured, your digital fingerprints last a lifetime. Also your video stories can last a lifetime on platforms like YouTube.

Indelible video impressions will live on beyond the tailgate so it's a good idea to plan for social media in ways tat serve to strengthen, simplify, and/or amplify your tailgating social media presence in ways that work for you and your family. Here are a few concepts to consider:

- Setting up a social media area—a banner with your tailgate name alongside it and the logos of the different sponsors goes a long way.

- Acknowledge that people have their cameras on their phones, and they can publish anything at any time. This is a friendly reminder to keep your sense and sensibilities intact.

- Don't do things you wouldn't want the world to see.

- Don't be the one filming others when they happen to be doing things they wouldn't want the rest of the world to see.

- If you do film something, do not share it. Even sharing with a dozen of your closest tailgaters is, effectively, the same as post-ing to the world wide web. It's called world wide for a reason.

- Do take pictures of the good times, and share those!

- Set your Facebook filter settings to approve any pictures that you are tagged in so that you will be able to review the photos that appear on your feed. Note: this will NOT keep the photos from appearing on other people's feeds.

Successful integration of social media into the tailgating lifestyle is important for your relationships. Knowing that the constant stimuli of social media will align quite strongly with and as a key trait of the likely attendees of your tailgates—type-A competitive personalities--is important to consider.[31] In the 1990s, tailgating involved five hours of talking to each other. Now, one second of downtime turns into the posting of a photo, a tweet, a text, or at least checking what someone's friends and what they are doing on their social media accounts.

Accordingly, and definitively, we're past a point of no return for social media in tailgating and in your relationships. Accepting that can help move the conversation forward.

A few years back, Cheryl's brother was in Cologne, Germany, for Thanksgiving. We set up Skype and interacted with him via a laptop as if he had a seat at the table. He was eight hours away, but he, literally, seemed like he was with us for Thanksgiving dinner before we watched the Aggies play that day. Not quite as good, but nearly as good, as the original. He had shared his time with us without all the expense and aforementioned issues of traveling. Think about the cost of the international airline ticket alone. There was no eight-hour flight—each way--or customs agent or lost luggage or anything else. Just eight hours of time spent together as a family.

With a global pandemic in play it's even more important to consider when, if and how social media will play a part in future social settings and sports gatherings. Zoom tailgates anyone?

Now, fast-forward to a tailgate in which similar dynamics are in play. First, there's the expense of the game ticket. Or even if you do not have a ticket to the game, you still have to find a parking pass or secure an Uber to get in and out. Arriving is only half the battle. Departures are decidedly more difficult in an Uber or Lyft situation on game days.

Not unlike our Thanksgiving via Skype, you can check a Facebook Live or Snap Story and feel very connected. It's almost as if you are at the tailgate or in the stands or watching the band perform. Someone else can tweet about the food they are eating and another can Instagram the drinks they are having without having to contend with the traffic or the earth, or wind, or fire—see Chapter 3 on how to best survive the elements.

After the amazing Alabama tailgate, one of our sponsors bought us industrial strength fans—seemingly 60" fans to match our 60" TVs—because it was so hot at the tailgate with no wind when he attended. He helped us solve a problem, but wouldn't it arguably have been easier to NOT deal with the problem by living vicariously through someone else's social media?

The bonding and the relationships you can establish with your family, friends, and tailgaters are arguably greater, but the experience is being compromised by the instant accessibility of it all.

As we look at the current state of affairs, companies like Apple are starting to provide smartphone details via your Settings on a section called "Screen Time"—found in iOS 12 or greater.

Are you spending three hours a day or more on your phone?

Are you checking your phone 80, 90, or 100 times a day? If you are knowledgeable about where you are, then how does your family fit in? Where do your friends come in? And how does this impact the tailgate?

Giving your relationships, your undivided attention, while ignoring your phone, is becoming increasingly difficult to do, but it's well worth it. Check how much you're really using your phone. If you're using it to "check out" during social occasions, we recommend that you "check in" to the real time and the real people near you, even if in a socially distant way.

Cheryl's Thoughts

The phone is important for communication purposes. A necessary evil and a huge benefit to keeping us connected on a grander scale.

The whole point is to be there and create a positive shared history. I like to use the phone to take planned pictures. I'm appreciative of all the pics like that people shared through the years.

In hindsight most people didn't spend time all that much time on their phones—now that I think of it—at the early tailgates. You can have real conversations with real people. I kind of wonder why people would waste so much of that valuable time on their phones.

There is also a group of people I would only catch up with during the tailgate season. We called them "tailgate friends."

Social media helped me stay connected to their lives during the off-season, but I much more enjoyed interacting with them during the season. Being a real person and leaving the phone alone allowed me to spend real time with them.

More than one person would say to me, "Your husband has a digital marketing agency and you aren't on Facebook?" I didn't even know when I joined Facebook—until Jim just looked. I joined Facebook on September 24, 2012 during the first SEC football season. I also just learned via Facebook that I was friends with Ellen Yelton before I was friends with my husband. True story. Also, her now-husband Joel Yelton and Jim were Aggie Stormtroopers for one of our Halloween tailgates. The game was against Texas Tech, and Zach dressed as Chewbacca. Great friends. Great times. Great memories.

Back then, trying to explain to accomplished, educated people what was going on with social media was interesting. At that point it was not completely mainstream. Jim's first book, *Car Dog* (published in 2015) was pretty interesting. There were many chapters about social media and how people feared it.

I got the hang of Facebook pretty quickly and love the family pictures. One of our family friends—because she is a friend and family member—Anna Lovoi was married to her husband Justin in December 2012. She and Jim did a Heisman Trophy pose at their wedding because Johnny Football had recently won the Heisman trophy.

At the end of the day, I prefer one-to-one interactions. While I appreciate the ability to stay connected in today's busy society via social media, I'll leave the posting--for the most part--to others.

Beyond the Tailgate: Timing matters. Choose when to train. Choose when to be "actively social" versus being on "social media." If you're missing the actual experience of an occasion due to excessive time on your phone, take a different path.

CHAPTER 12

❧

Take It to the Clubhouse

Our View

With the movement into the SEC, a freshly polished Heisman Trophy in tow, and a top five national ranking to boot, the Texas A&M Board of Regents approved a $485 million rebuild of Kyle Field in May of 2013.

A complete timeline is detailed to reinforce how expectations grew in Aggieland based on their early success. The innocent climb of early success was quickly being replaced with a need to escalate the commitments and capitalize on the newfound experience of winning on a national scale. The early run had been invigorating.

The stadium renovation finished just before the 2015 season and brought the official stadium capacity to 102,733. In the interim, capacity was actually greater than the current capacity due to more compressed seating arrangements. The construction plan was broken into multiple phases.

Phase I (November 2013): Demolition of the first deck of the east side of the stadium, reconstruction of the first deck, and construction of the south end zone, which included seating, media interview areas, 12th Man Productions and related game-day support, and a commissary and recruiting area.

Phase II (November 2014): Demolition of the entire west side of the stadium, complete construction of the south end zone, and reconstruction of the west side.

Other significant items included in the scope of work for the Kyle Field redevelopment included:

Demolition of the Read Building, G. Rollie White Coliseum, and the Netum Steed strength and conditioning facility, all of which are adjacent to or part of Kyle Field.

Construction of a new strength and conditioning training area on the university's west campus.

Lowering of the playing field by approximately seven feet and relocating the playing surface approximately 18 feet to the south, allowing for an additional six rows of seating around the stadium.

Relocation of the existing south end zone scoreboard and video board, reusing appropriate components to provide a scoreboard facility on the exterior of the north end zone structure: New interior scoreboard locations westablished in the south end zone and the northeast and northwest corners of the developed stadium.

Construction of wider tree-lined walkways along both sides of Houston Street from George Bush Drive to the stadium east mall area.

The new "South Side Upper Level" with an addition of an upper seating deck and concourse, with an estimated seating capacity of 12,000 and the potential of an additional 7,000 seats in the future, with seating to be located both below and above the upper concourse.[32]

With every new brick that was laid and every new tree that was planted, expectations increased. Having been through one conference transition already—from the Southwest Conference to the Big XII—A&M seem well prepared for the transition. Moreover, we watched as TCU moved from the Southwest Conference to the Western Athletic Conference, to Conference-USA, to the Mountain West Conference before finally joining the Big 12, and I found there to be two common threads. First, while the novelty of new conferences are exceptionally intoxicating, the reality is that the uniqueness of new conference opponents wears off quickly. Second, expectations increase as the size of the stadium increases.

In the Big 12, eagerly anticipated conference match-ups with Oklahoma were replaced with seemingly more frequent yet less appealing football games against Kansas and Kansas State. Now in the SEC, the games with the Mississippi schools might not be as intriguing over time as they would originally be. Knowing this, the Aggies not only built better seats, they built better suites. In the new construction, they built in every imaginable modern convenience, save for a retractable roof.

The university also constructed an impressive club level, and for the first time offered the opportunity to purchase adult beverages and food in the comfort of an air-conditioned environment. These upgrades changed more than the tailgating scene. It changed the coaching scene too.

A&M's debut in the SEC was incredibly impressive and the Aggies had a new stadium to show for it. Their head coach at the time, Kevin Sumlin, also capitalized on early success.

When he joined the Aggies, Sumlin's deal was for five years at $2 million a year. After an incredible first year in the SEC, his contract was extended a year, and the base was bumped to $3.1 million a year. One year after that, he signed a five-year $30 million deal. Stadium improvements and top-ranked recruiting classes were coming more quickly than anyone could have imagined.[33]

It went too far too fast for Sumlin, though, as the stadium resources and recruiting prosperity did not translate into additional success on the field. In November 2017 Sumlin was fired and moved to the University of Arizona. In an interesting bit of trivia, Sumlin was actually the nation's highest paid coach in 2018. Nick Saban received $11.1 million to coach Alabama; however, Sumlin received an astounding $12.4 million—$10.4 million from his Aggie buyout and $2.0 more million from the Arizona Wildcats.

The tailgate scene carries on despite all the university changes, but it, too, has evolved and continues onward, upward, and, not coincidentally, indoors. How Covid-19 changes all that will be determined somewhere beyond the tailgate.

Prior to the upgrades, Kyle Field was often referred to as a "tackle box." Indeed, it was not too fancy of a place to see a game. There were no seat backs prior to the stadium upgrade, and the all-aluminum benches forced fans to stand sideways to view the action. It's an Aggie tradition and an honor to stand during the football games. You stand for the whole game if you are a current student because you—just like former student E. King Gill—are ready to go into the game if or when needed.[34]

Former students also stand during key moments of the game, and in the tackle-box days, we stood sideways. Exactly 17" of seating was provided for each person in the lower levels and 15" in the upper levels. To stay with the fishing analogy, we were literally packed in like sardines.

On December 21, 2014, the iconic West Stands of Kyle Field were demolished in a planned detonation. By opening day in 2015, the all-new Kyle Field had seats with not only armrests but 21" of expansive room and comfort.

We, too, were growing as the Aggies were growing, and as such, decided to, in the process, turn over leadership of the Varsity Tailgates to the outstanding group of students who were just graduating. Chris, Cameron, Joshua, Teddy, Marty, and Lauren, and both Lindsay's contributed a great deal of time, energy, and resources throughout their years in school, as well as to their time just after graduation.

The team had enjoyed the unprecedented experience of participating, literally, in a once-in-a-lifetime growth into the SEC experience along with the associated highs and lows of tailgating. As it turned out, the former students did a great job, and the momentum of the SEC carried the team for several years; however, something happened along the way. They started to make life choices: many married—a few, as mentioned earlier, to each other. Some moved out of College Station to start careers. Others started graduate degrees. The camaraderie--while foundational--started to move beyond the tailgate. Social media became more accessible. You could somewhat *be there* without *being there.*

We offered every bit of support and attended almost every tailgate in the first few years, but the students turned adults were starting to understand how much advance preparation was required for tailgating at a Varsity level. They already knew it was no small operation. And while it's not at the peak level that it was once, the shared history carries on today in these pages as well as in real life.

The actual Varsity Tailgate carries on today thanks in large part to Vince Trahan and his wife, Becky. Jeff, Jenny, and Austin Trahan, among others, keep things going in a more comfortable location just off of the shaded doorways of Reed Arena.

Thanks to all the Varsity Tailgaters throughout the years and to those well in the future!

Cheryl's Thoughts

I won't belabor the point. By building the new stadium the transition to something bigger was very natural. It was a conversation starter about what was next, and it was a game changer for us, too.

Much like when families grow, other things on our calendar

became more demanding too. Going to and preparing for every game was no longer possible.

We also were able to meet Chastity Carrigan '16, who helped change our perspective on how we could stay active with the University. It certainly served as a catalyst for creating another scholarship through this book.

There's typically more than one thing that helps someone transition from one place to another from one phase to another.

I like how the tailgate has transitioned even without us there. It became what I wanted it to be: it's a family, and we are welcomed and can still see everybody. What a great experience we all shared!

And I knew—when we had our 25th wedding anniversary— that it meant something more because the overwhelming majority of people we celebrated with had been to our tailgates. In fact, before the anniversary event, Jim reminded me that we were "just going to a fancy tailgate." I smiled, and it made me feel better because I knew we would be with family and friends.

Joel Yelton, at the anniversary reception, reminded my nephews that he was the one who had dressed up in the Stormtroopers outfit for them during the Mizzou game in October 2010! They were 10 and 8 years old at the time. Now, as college-aged adults they broke into huge smiles and will likely continue to do so for the rest of their lives.

I still get a ton of "Remember when's?" and it's always nice to bond and reconnect over a good tailgating story

Beyond the Tailgate:

Life, much like the tailgate, is incredibly fluid, and you get to make adaptations. It is amazing and wonderful how relationships are sustained beyond the tailgate. Experience is a great teacher, too. Knowing when to say, "Good-bye," is just as important to family and friends' relationships as knowing when and how to say, "Howdy!"

Call to Action for Beyond the Tailgate Readers

Reviews can be difficult to come by and mean so much to authors. If you find yourself enjoying the book, please go to Amazon.com and type in "Beyond the Tailgate" to leave a review. Even if it's just one sentence about what you liked, the feedback is greatly appreciated. Feel free to email us and let us know if you've left a review. Either at jimflint12@gmail.com or cherflint94@gmail.com.

If you'd like to read or listen to other books by Jim please go to Amazon and look for *Car Dog Millionaire: How to Sell Cars and Make Money at Your Internet Dealership* or check out *20/20 Vision: Actionable Insights for Digital Retailers*.

EPILOGUE

*O*ur many thanks to everyone who participated in the tailgates.

We were honored then and are honored now to have been part of your lives. To our family, friends, and all those who participated, we were part of something bigger than ourselves.

We hope the memories and experiences live on *Beyond the Tailgate* in your eyes, hearts, minds and in these pages forever.

You can't lose when you're loved by so many!

OTHER BLOGS: TAILGATINGIDEAS.COM

*T*hroughout the pages of the book I endeavored to integrate portions of blogs and, in some instances, the blogs in their entirety.

However, if you're still looking for more great content, more details follow. In the next section I provide each blog in its complete format with it's approximate publication date.

This includes some blogs of product reviews that were not shared in the previous pages. Note: some of the products described here may or may not still be available for sale.

Enjoy!

The Top 12 for Varsity Tailgating Crew After 30 Games (Published 2010)

1 7 up and 13 down.

That's the Texas A&M won-loss record for games that I've attended. The .567 winning percentage for our crew would be good enough to get most college coaches relieved of their coaching responsibilities.

So why am I keeping up with Texas A&M games that our tailgate crew has attended? I recently became inspired by Rusty Burson's article in the *12th Man Magazine* about the Top 60 moments in the last 60 years for Aggie Athletics. As such, I've poured over our games and arrived at the Top 12 tailgating moments for our Varsity Tailgating crew.

#12: Saving the Best for Last – 11-26-09 vs. University of Texas – 39 to 49 Loss

Our most recent tailgate was the best. The weather cooperated, and on Thanksgiving Day, family, friends, and fried turkeys made for a great day of tailgating. If A&M had won, it would have been even better, but as the last tailgate of last year, it left everyone looking forward to next year. Moreover, when Jerrod Johnson outplayed Colt McCoy he renewed hopes in Aggieland that things are going to get better and soon.

#11: Pro Potential – 09-27-03 vs. University of Pittsburgh – 26 to 37 – Loss

In the process of one of the most dominating games I've ever seen by a wide receiver, Larry Fitzgerald ended up with seven catches for 135 yards and three TDs at Kyle Field. The highlight of the day included an over the shoulder catch that would even leave Willie Mays shaking his head. Although I've attached it here, I try not to watch the video too much because it diminishes the memory of seeing it live.

Normally, you hate to lose...Fitzgerald was so good though, you not only accepted that he was at another level, you were best served to appreciate it as well.

#10: The Heat Wave – 09-17-2005 vs. SMU – 66 to 8 – Win

Our first game as season ticket holders heated up way too quick.

In Texas you hear people from the Arizona talking about dry heat. On this day it was simply too hot for words. The Heat Index on the field had to be closer to 150 than to 100 and there was absolutely no wind. Just sitting in the stadium made me dizzy.

At the start of the third quarter, there were no less than 2,000 sweat stained people sitting in the air-conditioned area just outside of the Memorial Stadium Center bookstore in order to beat the heat.

#9: Hurricane Season –09-22-2005 – vs. Southwest Texas State – 44 to 31 – Win

Our second game as season ticket tailgaters got moved up to Thursday night, and it had nothing to do with ESPN. Hurricane Rita forced a change in schedule and resulted in a half-empty stadium.

Full disclosure: I watched this game on TV and ended up giving the tickets to some buddies who proceeded to go to College Station and tailgate throughout the game. Some of their updates from the evening's festivities would make even the most hard-core "Texts from Last Night Fan" blush.

Later they ended up at the Dixie Chicken and helped extend the Chicken's position as the national leader for bars in the most alcohol consumed per square foot of real estate.

#8: The Real Hurricanes Hit –09-20-2008 – vs. Miami Hurricanes – 23 to 41 – Loss

The Miami game was soo hyped. The game was soo light. Speed kills. Miami skill position players ran circles around A&M defenders.

#7: Name Change–08-30-2008 – vs. Arkansas State – 14 to 18 – Loss

For two years we called our tailgate team the "Silver Oak on the

Brazos." If the Aggies won, and since College Station is just off the Brazos River, we'd open up Silver Oak at the postgame tailgate. Great times.

On the drive up for the first game of the 2008 season, one of our newest tailgaters, Sarah, pointed out the window and said, "Hey, we should change our tailgate name. It looks like Silver Oak on the Brazos is a retirement community. That's pretty lame."

Sure enough, whatever self-perceived cool factor we had been working with had just been destroyed.

Not so cool of her too mention, but oh so true. The moment turned out to be the equivalent jinx of someone talking about a no-hitter during the middle of a baseball game.

Later that evening...somehow...some way...Texas A&M managed to lose to Arkansas State in Coach Mike Sherman's debut by committing four turnovers. When the last of those turnovers occurred with seven seconds left in the game—right in front of our seats—the silence was powerful. The shockwave that went through the stadium was palpable and made my head hurt and ears ring.

Our Silver Oak stayed on wraps that night and we began the process of renaming our tailgating team in earnest.

Top Tailgates for Texas A&M Tailgating Crew–Part Deux
(Published 2010)

*A*few weeks back, Rusty Burson's countdown in the *12th Man Magazine's* Top 60 moments in the last 60 years of Aggie Athletics inspired me. While it's over a much shorter time period, I've now detailed the Top 12 tailgating moments (good and bad) for our Texas A&M tailgating crew.

In a previous post I walked through numbers 12 through 7. Now for the Top 6.

#6: The Game Isn't Over–10-14-2006 – vs. Missouri Tigers – 25 to 19 – Win

On a perfect-weather day, in a game that the Aggies should have arguably lost, Texas A&M held on to beat the #21 ranked Missouri Tigers.

The real game ball goes to the postgame activity though. Legendary Texas Sportswriter Dan Cook of the *San Antonio Express-News* once wrote, "It ain't over 'til the fat lady sings."

For the first time, the tailgating crew participated in karaoke after the game.

#5: And Still Undefeated – 10-29-2005 – vs. Iowa State – 14 to 42 – Loss

The Texas A&M Fightin' Aggie Band ALWAYS wins halftime. In a 2005 game vs Iowa State, A&M was down 21-14 at halftime. A couple of us were ready to head back to the tailgate toward the end of the first half. Things were already looking bad in what ultimately turned out to be a ho-hum 5-6 campaign.

However, we decided to stay. The Aggie band performs with such precision, and they are mesmerizing to watch. Check out this video from A Few Good Men, which actually is the Texas A&M Aggie Corp of Cadets band members.

After the band won halftime, we left with an idea that we could make it back to our seats later in the game. Unfortunately, our tailgate team and the Aggies never came back. Final score 42-14. We stayed at the tailgate for the rest of the day and evening and night and into the morning. A bad game, ironically, resulted in a great tailgate.

#4: Back-to-Back the Right Way – 11-23-2007 – vs. Texas – 38 to 30 – Win

Midway through the middle of 2007 we decided that we were going to provide a jersey to my wife for all the pregame meals and the little things that added up to big things that she was taking care of for the crew. We were hoping to give her the jersey on a game that we thought we could win, but in an up-

and-down season, we started to run out of dates.

As the final game approached we discussed postponing the ceremony until the following year because we expected that the Longhorns—after having lost to us the prior year in Austin—would be sufficiently motivated to return the favor in College Station. It had been a long year for Coach Franchione—what with the email scandal and all—and even though many felt like the only way he could save his job was with a win over the #11 Longhorns they were heavy favorites as they rolled into Kyle Field.

The guys presented the jersey in a pregame ceremony, we had a great tailgate and then walked over to the game expecting that it would be a long night. The game ended up being a shocker and the jersey a good luck charm. Ironically, on our way home we found out that Coach Fran—despite back-to-back wins over our archrivals—had been fired.

#3: Back-to-Back the Wrong Way – 11-04-2006 vs. Oklahoma – 16 to 17 – Loss and 11-11-07 vs. Nebraska – 27 to 28 – Loss

ESPN's *College GameDay* came to town for the first of back-to-back night games at Kyle Field for a game against Oklahoma. We arrived early that day and found a GREAT, new tailgating spot—or so we thought.

The grass WAS greener than our traditional spot AND the new location had much, much more tailgating room. We could throw footballs around. We were closer to the stadium. The portable restrooms were nearby and clean. We thought we had found one of the best places tailgating locations on campus. It took us two weeks to find out we were in the wrong place.

Late in the 4th quarter of a closely contested, smash-mouth football game, Coach Franchione opted to kick a field goal on the 4th and less than a yard—despite having the 6'0", 295-pound Jorvorskie Lane available.

A monster of a man, the guy's nickname is J-Trane because he favors a locomotive and because that's what it feels like when you try to tackle him.

The field goal cut the lead to one. Later in the 4th, with about two minutes remaining, Oklahoma head football coach Bob Stoops, choose a different path and went for it on 4th and 2 on his own side of the field AND converted. The 12th Man at Kyle Field was oh so loud and the game oh so close, but a day and a tailgating location filled with promise ended on a solemn note ad a one-point loss.

A week later, we came back to the exact same tailgating spot. Timing and good fortune were ours. We thought we had found a new tailgating home.

Unfortunately, though, the sick feeling from the week before returned when Texas A&M missed an extra point on a touchdown. These things have a tendency to catch up with you.

Later, Maurice Purify from Nebraska made a leaping, twisting catch on a pass from Zac Taylor with 21 seconds left on the clock to tie the game. The extra point won the game.

Back-to-back one-point losses in what ended up being a 9-4 season.

Normally after a game we stay at the tailgate to let the

traffic clear out. Not this time. We broke down our equipment in record time and sat in the traffic—stunned by back-to-back one-point losses. While we waited, we agreed that we would never set foot upon our new tailgate spot ever again.

#2: Triple OT, Moving Stadiums, and Rainbows – 09-08-2007 vs. Fresno State – 47-45 – Win

In what promised to be an uneventful game, the Bulldogs and Aggies battled in a Triple OT thriller. It happened to be the first tailgate where we encountered rain. We learned that a game plan for electronic equipment is important. We didn't lose any equipment, but we had to hustle.

Thanks to the showers, a rainbow materialized over Kyle Field during the middle of the third quarter. What an amazing sight to see.

Overtime games are rare enough, but Triple OT plays out with so many twists and turns that it's incredible. As the OTs progressed, the student body started moving back and forth across the top deck of Kyle Field to track the action. This video gives you an idea of what it looked like. I've never seen anything like it before or since.

After the game, back at the tailgate, one of our new tailgaters learned the powerful and painful lesson that tailgating is a marathon and not a sprint.

#1: We'll Be Back – 11-13-1993 vs. Louisville – 42 to 7 – Win

The first Texas A&M game that my wife and I attended was in 1993. We were engaged at the time and had the opportunity to pet Reveille VI—A&M's collie mascot—as a puppy during the game in which he took over for the retiring Reveille V.

Pregame tailgating didn't exist back then—especially like it does today—but there was the feeling that we'd be back. Almost 17 years later we're looking forward to our sixth season of Texas A&M tailgating.

From Nine(ty) to Five
(published 2010)

After a tough week at work the last thing you need is to be stressed out at your tailgate. Our Texas A&M tailgating crew has continued to improve each year by adding new items to the mix that help us enjoy the Aggies football season. Through the years we've added at least one key piece of equipment—a grill, a generator, even a TV. Typically, after the addition you wonder how you ever lived without the product before.

This year, after careful consideration, the big addition to our Texas-sized tailgate will be the Winegard Carryout – GM-1518. The Winegard is a fully automatic, portable satellite TV antenna.

In previous years, I've spent approximately 90 minutes per tailgate setting up the antenna in order to watch other football games during pre- and postgame.

When doing this manually it's more than threading a needle. It's more like threading the needle *after* finding it in the haystack. On more occasions than I'd care to mention, I've ended up on the phone with the Dish Network helpline working through some technical issue while family and friends enjoyed the tailgate.

Watching TV at tailgate is one of the best experience out there, but when it's taking your blood pressure to new heights it's time to look at new options.

In walks the Winegard Carryout.

What the azimuth?

To set up the antenna on your own you need to establish a level location, set the dish perfectly to triangulate three key angles—one of them being the hard to acquire azimuth—and then lock on the satellite. The weekly setup that I went through for two years made Harrison Ford's work in the map room during *Raiders of the Lost Ark* look like child's play.

One of my well-intentioned, buddies, a CPA in fact, wanted the TV at the tailgate as much as I did, and he tried to pitch in during satellite set up. However, he lasted about three weeks on the satellite assignment and asked to be reassigned—rather "promoted"—to grilling duty. While he loves the TV, he said that the whole process was too precise and reminded him way too much of his day-to-day accounting work.

Additionally, during a typical setup five to ten people would come by and ask how the system worked. Texas A&M is a friendly place with a strong engineering school. As a result, lots of well-intended, logical questions came from good-hearted, helpful Aggies. Truth be told, though, it's kind of stressful explaining what you're doing when it's not clear that you know what you're doing.

After checking back and forth on pricing and compatibility with Dish Network, I set my sites on the Winegard Carryout over the VuQube as I sought the solution to our satellite TV set-up problems.

Although, I typically had the TV working, this commercial isn't THAT far removed from our previous experiences...

Tailgating Tip: Be sure to have at least one test run at home before you take any system to game day so you can familiarize yourself with the equipment and the entire set-up process.

The First Test Run

After taking my Honda A2000 generator out of storage for its first work of the year and dusting off all the equipment, I went through the necessary steps of reactivating the Dish Network service, connecting the Winegard, and connecting the TV. As mentioned, it had previously taken me up to 90 minutes to get the satellite locked each week.

This time though it took me 90 minutes to get everything out of off-season ice and up and running. Full functionality was achieved, including time spent checking the spark plug for, the oil level of, and the gas level for the generator.

Accessory note: I purchased a 110v AC/DC converter for the Winegard on eBay so that I could run the unit off of my generator. The Winegard Carryout comes standard with a 12v cigarette lighter connector for use in most vehicles.

The Second Time

Now that I had the system working, I came back a few weeks later to see just how fast I could get everything going again.

I put the Dish Network receiver, the Winegard Carryout, the Honda generator, the Samsung TV, and all the wires on the ground in front of me without any completed connections. Then I started the timer on my iPhone and went to work. In less than five minutes the generator was purring, the wires were connected, and the satellite antenna was locked on. What a huge difference!

It took another four minutes for Dish Network to download the programming. All told, it took me nine minutes and 41 seconds to start surfing channels with my remote control.

What's Next?

So, the product and I are ready for tailgating in Aggieland. There's a difference though between the backyard and the tailgate parking lot, and I have, admittedly, a few more hurdles to clear.

First, I have to figure out how to elevate the Winegard. They sell a two-foot tripod; however, since we're in a high-traffic tailgating area that's a little removed (approximately 20 yards) from where we park, we could have intermittent transmission difficulties due to random people walking by.

For most parking-lot tailgating from the back of a truck or SUV, it would be easy enough to put the Winegard Carryout on top of your vehicle without any issues; however, that's not the case for us. In a parking-lot situation, though, I can't imagine a better scenario than plugging the 12v adapter into your car, placing the antenna on the roof, and watching the games. Almost too easy.

Also, they say the warranty is voided if I paint the dome, but I know that a custom maroon shell will play really well in College Station. Moreover, they sell a black dome as an accessory so I'm thinking there is a way around this.

If anyone has ideas or potential solutions on these topics please feel free to respond below.

Customer Service

The customer support line consists of one guy on call on Saturdays. No one works on Sundays, which could be a downer for NFL fans, but this guy—Kevin—has to be as lonely as the Maytag repairman. When we talked, he appeared to genuinely be pleased to be speaking with me. He noted that he mostly helps first-time users work through connection issues with either Dish Network or DIRECTV. As anyone who has researched this category knows, each company has its own demons, but Winegard really doesn't appear to be the kind of product that needs to have too much in the way of troubleshooters because the product, simply enough, works.

Product Specs

Details about the product can be found on Winegard's company website.

Detailed specs are also listed here for reference:

- Automatically find satellites – no remote or controls needed
- Lightweight and durable
- Easy grip handle for effortless carrying and security
- Standard programming: Dish Network, Bell TV and DIRECTV
- HD programming: Dish Network and Bell TV
- Supports up to 2 receivers
- Dimensions: 15.6" dome height, 20" diameter
- Unit Weight: 13.5 Pounds

Bottom Line

Is it worth the purchase price?

If you are looking for a game-changing experience, the answer is yes. If you have a grill and a generator or you just love watching football on game day this IS the absolute next step.

Satellite TV tailgater wannabes would be well served to start with this product too. You might save a few dollars by buying dish equipment or you could take the satellite off your house, but in most cases, the pain involved in any of those scenarios just doesn't make sense. Sure, I learned the hard way, but why not learn from my mistakes?

The real benefit to the product is how easy they've made a very, if not THE most, difficult part of tailgate setup. You may have some buddies who mean well, but when they are in the hot September sun and have the choice of grabbing an adult beverage from the cooler or helping you triangulate the TV, there really isn't much of a choice, is there?

Thanks to the Winegard Carryout I'll increase my available tailgating time by more than ten hours this season and reduce the stress level at the tailgate. Priceless.

GAMER BEVERAGE DISPENSER REVIEW (PUBLISHED 2011)

*B*ig Fan Tailgating shipped me a Gamer Beverage Dispenser to test out during the last two Texas A&M games. Timing was right to test and for the product launch. Two games, six days.

Upside: You Look Marvelous

The product looks great. The Dispenser, in fact, was the talk of the tailgate prior to the Texas A&M vs. Kansas game. People wanted to put the product through its paces.

The product simply looks stellar with wonderfully matched school colors and logos. To borrow from Billy Crystal's Fernando character of *Saturday Night Live* fame: "You look marvelous."

This I know: a true sports fan would be very excited to receive this product—it simply looks wonderful.

The Downside: Judging a Book Completely by Its Cover

While it looks great, my tailgate team had difficulties with the prototype unit that Big Game Tailgating provided to us for testing. The seal at the bottom leaked. The dispenser leaked more than the porous Kansas Jayhawk secondary who we saw on Kyle Field a few hours later during the Aggies 61-7 victory. The excitement we originally felt for the Dispenser went away in about 15 seconds when we realized the unit couldn't be used.

The leak problem was big enough that I let their president know about the issue first thing Sunday morning. The next day he sent me a note advising that they had inadvertently shipped me a preproduction sample for the Aggies Dispenser. The final Aggies unit, in its finished format, actually would not ship until mid-December.

To make it right and for more testing purposes, they sent me a Georgia replacement Dispenser. Exceptional customer service and a background that includes licensed big school products for Tailgate Tables, Washer Tosses, the Chill Stick, and many more tailgate-oriented items helped to set Big Fan Tailgating apart. Two days later I had the replacement helmet.

When the Georgia helmet arrived I quickly assembled the product—took five minutes—and then placed water in the container portion of the product. I wanted to be certain the water held overnight with no leaks at all. It did so with no problems.

So, while this background is important to mention, it seems that Big Game Tailgating has the seal issue solved. Moreover, any issues should be handled quickly and smartly via their customer support.

At first glance, the Dispenser looks like a blender. It's decidedly not. It is simply a very good-looking beverage dispenser. Title says so, but at a glance—both inside and outside the box—it's what you might mistake the product for being.

The base of the dispenser is solid and as another nice touch, the company provides a drip collector with a magnet base that smartly clings to and adjusts underneath the aforementioned tap.

In a segment all its own—the collegiate licensed dispenser is a product that makes sense. For many of us? We'll have to wait until collegiate licensed blenders become more widely available.

Final Recommendation

Gamer Beverage Dispenser, you look marvelous! Form sometimes trumps function in the tailgating world, and such is this case for this all-new product from Big Game Tailgating. If you are looking for a cool, new tailgating idea this holiday season, then this product comes through in the clutch.

Gameday Rugs –
It's Like a Flag
for Your Floor
(published 2010)

Gameday Rugs, a company founded earlier this year by Engineered Conversion Systems, delivers high-quality sports-licensed rugs and mats with college logos. The company, a division of Engineered Conversion Systems (ECS), is experienced and successful in product development for the carpet and rug industry. Their entry into the floor mat, rug, and doormat space is a logical extension of business that they know well.

When I received the rug, though, I just didn't think the product would be a logical extension into the tailgating space. Boy was I wrong.

First Impression

When I rolled out the Gameday Rug, I noticed the quality and liked the look. The high-caliber construction delivers sharp colors, firm tufts, and perfect logos. Each of these features connects tightly to a solid plastic backing that keeps the rug from slip-sliding away at your tailgate or in your home.

They shipped me this version to test at our tailgate.

It looked, to me, like a great doormat, but I didn't hold out much hope for success at our tailgate, and I felt a little bad about taking it to the tailgate. The look is luxurious enough to be used indoors and is clearly durable enough to be placed outside; I just didn't want to damage such an attractive product.

Moreover, I thought: *A rug at a tailgate?*

However, when I placed the welcome mat down, people noticed the rug. They liked the rug. They wanted to know where to get their own rug. In general, people like the addition and, to me, it symbolically served as a welcome mat to all the tailgaters who joined us that day.

This product would be even more effective and noticeable in a parking lot environment.

One of our visitors last weekend noted, "It's like a flag for your floor."

With the official school logo and superior construction, the team at Gameday Rugs has a great new way for avid tailgaters to display their school pride.

Tailgating with a rug? Who knew? It's now a welcome addition to our tailgating paraphernalia.

Ten Pound Clear View Propane Tank Review (Published 2012)

$\mathcal{I}$t was back in September 2010 when we discovered Clear View Propane Tanks. In a nutshell, Clear View Propane Tanks are translucent composite fiberglass propane tanks with a protective outer plastic casing. The major shift from holding and transporting propane in an old steel cylinder is that Clear View tanks are lighter weight, more portable, resistant to corrosion, and explosion proof. In addition to all that, the best part about these propane tanks is that you can actually see the level of propane inside, so you'll never have to guess how much propane you have left.

Since Clear View Propane Tanks were new to the United States in 2010, a limited quantity was available and in limited sizes. We received numerous emails from people saying they loved the Clear View tanks but were hoping to get them in a more "tailgate friendly" size. The Clear View tanks available at that time were the full-size cylinders that were comparable to the 20 lb. steel tanks you normally find at those propane exchanges. Tailgaters wanted something smaller, more compact, and lighter than the full size, but also wanted the benefits of being able to tell how much propane is left before needing to refill. The folks at Ragasco, the distributor of the Clear View Propane Tank brand, heard the tailgaters loud and clear. They recently introduced the smaller and even lighter 10 lb. tanks and we got one of the first tanks in order to review it.

The 10 lb. Clear View tank is shorter than the 20 lb. tank we reviewed over a year ago. Even though that is the main difference, it makes a big difference to us tailgaters. The 10 lb. version is much lighter and allows for more room in your car. Honestly, the 20 lb. tank was great for the peace of mind of knowing that no matter how long you cooked in the parking lot, you wouldn't run out of fuel. The 10lb. little brother provides the same assurance. If you are cooking for such a long time that you are using up ten pounds of propane at one tailgate, your grill must be cooking up a ton of food for a lot of people.

Seeing that we got ourselves a 10 lb. Clear View tank, we had to test it out. It performed just like the 20 lb. version that we still have from over a year ago, but just in a smaller package. It was lighter and fit in the back of my SUV better, taking up less room. I took it tailgating the previous weekend and used it to fire up the grill before a college baseball game. I enjoyed the peace of mind of knowing that I was not going to run out mid-cook and also could see the level of propane inside as the grill was burning.

All in all, if you read the review from over a year ago of the 20 lb. Clear View Propane Tank, you would think they couldn't have improved the product, in my opinion. They did and by making it smaller yet still holding plenty of propane, they improved the product with us tailgaters in mind. We would highly recommend the 10 lb. Clear View Propane tank to any tailgater who prefers cooking with liquid propane gas while out in the parking lot.

Auto-mo-brella
Tailgating Review
(Published 2010)

*D*o you remember the Brockabrella?

When Lou Brock, the Hall of Fame outfielder with the St. Louis Cardinals, wasn't collecting stolen bases and base hits, he was out hawking the Brockabrella. Today, he's still lovingly remembered in the Midwest and across America for lending his name to this unique sun-protecting device.

Not to be outdone, Gene Mayfield, the inventor of the Auto-mo-brella, developed his own sun protecting device after attending a NASCAR race and watching people struggle with setting up their tailgating tents and umbrellas. Brock's umbrella protects your head. Mayfield's protects your car or truck.

Gene's company, GTM Products, now offers the Auto-mo-brella, an over-sized umbrella setup that works effectively for single-person operations that aren't looking to struggle with the complexities of setting up a multi-man tent.

Want a Little Less Sun in Your Outdoor Fun?

The product is, essentially a high-quality, lightweight

umbrella that easily locks into the back of your SUV or truck as a telescoping tailgating hitch. The device creates much needed shade and the umbrella pivots to protect you from the elements—no matter the time of day. It's a simple one-person setup and tear down–a process that went smoothly when I put the product through its paces.

There are a few requirements, though. First, you'll need a class-two trailer hitch. Additionally, you'll need to plan to tailgate in a parking-lot environment right behind where you park.

Deciding to allocate a precious trailer hitch is a big deal. Many of you have followed in Dave's footsteps and built out your own tailgating grill. You'll have to make the call on the priority for your tailgate.

For those who have other designs for the tailgating hitch, a nice addition to the product would be a stand. Whether on a hitch or on the ground the Auto-mo-brella can provide much needed protection from the Texas sun. Our tailgating team talked about building one on our own so that we could protect our annexed grillers from the elements adjacent to our main tent.

The other prerequisite is a clear parking place. If you're on an area removed from your vehicle, this product won't make as much sense for you. If you're in a parking lot, though, it can be a great complement to your tailgating exploits. The unit smartly avoids conflicts with the rear lift or tailgate of your SUV or truck.

The Verdict?

Veteran football tailgaters won't be as interested in this product as new tailgaters. The logoed tailgating tent is a staple of tailgating pride, and while it's a little more expensive, it's an important addition to football tailgating activities.

The product works well and as described, but the price point doesn't make it attractive enough to recommend. There aren't any complaints about the product. It's high quality, and it will help you take your tailgating to the next level. However, there's another level just around the corner, and it can be reached for close to the same price.

Other Options?

The company is moving aggressively in the tailgating space. They have two other products including a tailgate umbrella with and a tailgate party mate that functions as a picnic table. They appear to be sturdy enough to withstand the most aggressive tailgating environment, just like the product I tested.

Thirst Down's Water Bottle: Solid, but not Tailgate Approved
(PUBLISHED 2010)

*T*hirst Down, Inc.: Great company name for someone in the football rehydration category.

"Go Ahead and Let Our Team Promote Your Team": Great tagline and fits nicely into what the company can effectively do.

"The Only Real Football Water Bottle": Another great catchphrase, but as Lee Corso might say, "Not so fast my friend."

With a chance to review Thirst Down's entry into the football bottle category, things looked promising. At first glance it appeared that Thirst Down might have cracked the code on inserting a water bottle into the central portion of a Nerf, while maintaining the integrity of the football. What a great idea with potential for lots of fun across the tailgating parking lots of America. Ideas for tailgating games started to come to mind.

However, when the product arrived, the first tagline rang truer: "Go Ahead and Let Our Team Promote Your Team." The plastic, football-shaped water bottle provides room for companies or football teams to proudly display their logos.

Of the two versions I received—one with a lanyard and one without—the one with the lanyard seemed to have more potential. A water bottle with a lanyard isn't as cool as a Super Bowl lanyard with tickets around your neck per se, but I could see children using the lanyard on the sidelines at youth football league games—think flag football leagues, not tackle.

Another reason the lanyard version worked more effectively? The non-lanyard version doesn't stand up by itself. Stay with me on this. you fill your plastic football with water and place it on a table, only to find that it's weeble-wobbled its way off the table top and onto the ground for a splash landing.

At most tailgates you need to have a place to set your drink down. This product doesn't allow for that fundamental necessity.

The detailed pebble grain of the bottle, as well as the plastic laces, demonstrate a certain attention to detail that the company held to in the development of the product. As a promotional platform it does have a clean surface for the addition of logos—almost exactly where an NFL or NCAA logo would go. Another very nice touch.

If Thirst Down develops a way to have the "bottle" stand upright or to make the product's exterior more Nerf-like, they might have something for the tailgating crowd. Until then, Thirst Down's product will serve youth football leagues and promotional events more effectively.

GARPEPANO SPICE
(PUBLISHED 2010)

At every Houston Astros home game, the Taco Bell Hot Sauce Race brings fans to their feet. Fire Sauce, Hot Sauce, and Mild Sauce sprint around the edge of the field in foul ball territory to determine the winner.

So far this year, only Hot Sauce and Fire Sauce have been in the winner's circle. Mild Sauce remains winless and as the lovable loser.

A product I recently reviewed, because of its surprisingly spicy characteristics, lands in the winner's circle as well.

We took Garpepano Spice—marketed as a great at-home tailgating spice for everyone's favorite tailgating food, PIZZA, to task during a recent poolside party.

Guests from San Antonio, where they like their hot sauce spicy and their salsa on fire, helped us test the product. I've traveled to the East Coast on many occasions, and the food tends to be less spicy than what I've found in Texas (think salsa) and New Orleans (think Cajun). During our testing, we were pleasantly surprised to discover that this Baltimore-based company developed a product with some serious kick.

The spice didn't quite start the eyes watering or noses running, but it definitely had pop. As the flavor settled through, it didn't feel too heavy, and it brought out the Italian flavors in the pizza via the mix of herbs and cheeses found in the spice.

For comparative purposes, we put Garpepano up against the Papa John's spice that comes standard with your pizza order. The Papa John's mix delivered an extremely salty experience. Upon further inspection, and as one might expect, sodium happened to be the leading ingredient in the Papa John's mix. By comparison, the more complex Garpepano Spice delivered a much better taste experience.

THE MADDEN CURSE
FOR DREW BREES
(PUBLISHED 2010)

*F*or the last several years we've hooked up our Xbox at the tailgate and played the upcoming game on the TV screen before the game is actually played in the stadium. Every year we look forward to finding out who graces the EA Sports cover of the Madden NFL and NCAA football video games.

In 2010, the Saints brought hope to downtrodden sports franchises everywhere.

But did you hear the news? For Madden 2011, Drew Brees is on the cover.

Saints fans just remember when the game comes out and you buy your copy, the season is already over. The "Madden Curse" lives on in New Orleans this year.

The Curse started with Madden 2000 when EA Sports agreed to a license with the NFL Players Association and decided that it would be a great idea to put Barry Sanders in the background of the standard John Madden photo. Inexplicably, before he even played a game that season, Sanders retired from football. He never played again.

Whoa, New Orleans...a city that already believes in the supernatural...a city that has more voodoo shops per capita than any place in the world...now has to deal with the curse of all curses. The *"Sports Illustrated* Jinx" has nothing on what Madden brings.

Check out this partial list:

- In 2004 Michael Vick landed on the cover of Madden. One day after the video game hit retail shelves he broke his right fibula in a preseason game. He didn't play that year. Several years later he landed in jail for dogfighting.

- In 2008 Vince Young, coming off an all-pro season, missed the first games of his LIFE due to injury. The first game ever—junior high, high school, college, or pro. The next year, the Texas Longhorn standout ended up on Coach Jeff Fisher's bench, as well as his suicide watch list.

- In 2009 Brett Favre graced the cover as a Packer. He never played another down with Green Bay, as he ended up playing for the Jets. We know the drama that happened then and still continues.

The city had to see it coming when they set up the online voting in February; it wasn't enough that Brees could win, it's that EA Sports stacked the deck so heavily in his favor. Fans could vote for Reggie Wayne, Jared Hamilton, or Brees. Really, who else could win? This was preordained. If Saints fans would have known about the Curse, they would have voted for "Other" by the thousands.

But they didn't. So, Saints fans, enjoy the Super Bowl and the associated glory. There just isn't any chance of back-to-back Super Bowl action here. In fact, none of the superstars featured on the cover of EA Sports have ever gone on to win another Super Bowl. That's right; no one who has ever appeared on the cover has subsequently won the big game again.

You look at the window they climbed through last year and it makes sense that they might have peaked. Once you're at the pinnacle there's truly nowhere else to go but down.

And the fates were pretty gracious to the team. First, a first-round bye after losing the last three games of the year. Then a lay down game against the Cardinals and a follow-up against the Vikings that they should have lost—save for Brett Favre throwing another season-ending interception.

After the interception in the NFC Championship, they choose wisely during the overtime flip of the coin. So wisely, in fact, that the NFL subsequently changed their entire playoff overtime rules. Only then did a relatively unheard-of kicker nail a 40-yard field goal that was put into place by a once-in-a-century pass interference call. A little good karma to say the least.

During the Super Bowl it took an onside kick and a Manning pick to steal the win.

And know this, I want the Saints to win as much or more than any team. This isn't an ominous curse in a "Glad this is happening kind of way to an evil franchise" like one might have felt for the Bad Boy Pistons of the early '90s. This is much more an "Uh-oh hate to see bad things happen to a franchise that's been through so much," like when the ball rolled through Bill Buckner's legs.

My dad has season tickets, and we've gone to a Saints game each year for the last decade or so. There's greatness at the Superdome, so it's with great sadness that I acknowledge that bad things are headed the Saints way. I grew up in Biloxi watching Archie Manning, Chuck Muncie, and Wes Chandler. Saints fans, there's lots of love here.

Could the Madden Curse really extend to a city though? I'm sorry, NOLA, but the answer is YES, and it's already started.

Is it coincidence that bad things have happened so quickly? Not to Brees per se...YET, but the city and region are already taking hits.

The BP oil spill is wreaking havoc on New Orleans and the Louisiana coast. The disaster now trumps the Exxon Valdez as the worst oil spill EVER, and its legacy will be felt years from now—if they can even get the problem solved. I don't mean to make a light of a terrible tragedy, but the Madden cover announcement and the oil spill happened within hours of each other.

It's worth considering, though, and either way we've watched 40+ days of an oil spill that's been like watching another hurricane hit a region that already knows way too much about hurricanes.

Then approximately ten days after the Madden cover announcement, Geoffrey Santini, a former Saints security director filed a lawsuit against head coach Sean Payton. The suit alleges that the Saints tried to cover up Payton's theft of Vicodin and other painkillers from the Saints' medical offices. Mr. Santini issued notice that he would file the lawsuit in September of last year, but it took a Madden cover to get the ball and the legal proceedings rolling.

I'm just saying...that's two national-level and noteworthy news events, and we're just turning the corner into June.

New Orleans is a great town. Bourbon Street is one of the best tailgate locations in the world, and Drew Brees is a great quarterback and leader of the city. However, now that Brees is on the cover of Madden 2011, he AND the city of New Orleans should be on the lookout.

Go Dish
(PUBLISHED 2010)

Two years ago, we introduced satellite TV to our tailgate. While it's a game changer, it's an expensive proposition to get started. In these tough economic times, how do you get the most bang for your buck?

I revisited the issue recently to make sure we had the best (1) sports programming options and (2) prices going into next season.

The premise: I called each factory 800 line for Dish Network and DirecTV, and in the interest of full disclosure, told them that I was writing a blog for TailgatingIdeas.com. As an avid Texas A&M tailgater, I wanted to determine the best options going into next season. To minimize expense, the tailgate TV satellite system needed to be operational for the 120 days of football tailgating.

Going in, without the NFL Sunday Ticket, the Dish Network is at a HUGE disadvantage. For NFL tailgaters that may be the only decision point. If not? Read on.

When I made the call and explained my tailgating goals, they quickly transferred me to the mobile satellite group, and I spoke with Hannah. She knew her stuff and recommended the Flex Program for tailgaters. Start anytime. Stop anytime. She knew her sports. She knew her business.

The monthly cost at the time of publication includes their Top 250 programming as well as HD versions of the NFL Network & NFL RedZone, Fox Sports, Local Channels, ESPN, ESPN2, ESPNU, and CBS College Sports and the Big Ten Network.

Buyer Beware: The Mountain West channel is not available and with TCU, Utah, and BYU reaching national prominence, this may mean that you will miss some Top 25 college action. ESPN Classic is not included either.

The ESPN College Game Plan is extra. Thankfully, Dish added the NFL RedZone, which should address concerns for fantasy footballers.

The call to Direct TV went on for an improbable 48 minutes. It felt like 48 hours.

After a quick transfer to their mobile division, I spoke with Matt—who didn't have knowledge of tailgating needs and was unable to identify a program that could work for me. His expertise was in the RV arena, and he ultimately transferred me back to the home sales division. There, Janette was friendly and well-intentioned, but lacked in knowledge as well. At one point she noted, "My computer isn't programmed for this. Hold on."

She turned me over to James, the floor supervisor. James knew his stuff, but in one phone call with three different employees I had received three different price quotes. I felt like a Florida linebacker trying to get a read on a Tommie Frazier triple-option play. Dazed and confused, I charged ahead.

On many occasions, they told me that I wasn't "allowed" to use the equipment in the manner I wanted to. Even though numerous DirecTV satellites are put into play, week after week, by Texas A&M tailgaters outside of Kyle Field. The company line for DirecTV is that they do not provide mobile satellite platforms outside of the RV division.

At the end of the conversation, James told me that I would actually have to buy two receivers, even though—get this–I wouldn't be using one of them. Who needs a receiver they aren't going to use? This call ended up being more lame duck than a four-loss Oregon team fighting for a berth in the Emerald Bowl. Simply stated, they just weren't able to address my tailgating needs.

The company held tight that the satellite would have to be installed at my house—no exceptions. Also, Direct TV continued to ask me when we could schedule the installation of the equipment at my house. Just like the University of Texas O-line facing Ndamukong Suh in the Big 12 Championship Game, I knew it was going to be a long night early on.

On the 120-day program the monthly rate climbed.

To his credit, James kept telling me that if I would only sign up for a 24-month contract I'd be getting a better deal. There would be no equipment fees and the first month would include all my sports packages.

However, the two-year price tag ran more than $1,800 and

with two years of Sunday Ticket, you end up passing the $2,500 mark. For the same amount you could have six years of the, admittedly, more limited Dish Network coverage.

The bottom line is to Go Dish.

Dish Network wins on price, customer service, and flexibility. DirectTV wins on NFL Sunday Ticket and the Mountain West Conference, but at a much higher total cost.

THE DESIGNATED SITTER
(PUBLISHED 2010)

*W*ith baseball season fast approaching, it brought to mind a new tailgating strategy we're looking to employ next year...the "Designated Sitter."

When it's game time, we just won't leave our most expensive electronic equipment and generators outside during the game. We've never lost a chair, a cooler, or any of the smaller items that we've left out at our tailgate. Texas residents know that Aggies don't lie, cheat, or steal. However, there are enough concerns about attendees from other schools, general collegiate mischief, and the occasional rain and wind, that we don't routinely leave our generators or TVs out for the taking. As a result, we have to set up, then break down our stuff before game time in order to be in our seats for kickoff. Then we have to do the same thing again once the game ends.

When we land at our tailgate spot, we move quickly to set the tent, tables, generators, TVs, satellite dishes, and food. Our crew goes from show up to setup in less than 30 minutes. It's a finely tuned precision unit pregame. Postgame? Not so much.

If our entire tailgate crew has seats, going into the stadium results in more than twice the work.

To that effect, over the last few years, I've missed more fourth quarters than I care to imagine—no matter the score. The reason? Who wants to come back to the tailgate and have to set up so many things again? Whether you want to drown your sorrows or celebrate a great win, it's nice to have everything ready for your arrival. Moreover, who doesn't want to see the scores of all the other games and maybe catch the ending of another great college game on TV. (Web browsing for scores by mobile phone isn't effective on game days in College Station. Too many people, not enough bandwidth.)

That's why, this year, we're moving to the American League of tailgating and becoming bigger fans of the Designated Sitter. Our plan is to have at least one person outside the stadium at the tailgate to watch the games on TV, play any tailgate games they like, and, basically, keep an eye on things.

Bottom line: With a Designated Sitter, our TOTAL set-up and break-down time goes from more than two hours total to less than 45 minutes. That extra time will be spent with family and friends and more tailgating fun. What a great trade off! Plus, the Designated Sitter can plan ahead and bring new tailgating friends or catch up with other like-minded tailgaters in the area.

So How Do You Choose?

Short of drawing straws, we're going to trade out Designated Sitters for the nonconference weekend, where time inside or outside the stadium won't be an issue. We'll also plan to trade out people at halftime so that everyone shares in the responsibility and the good times of tailgating and game watching.

If there is a huge game on the schedule, we may go back to the old setup of break-it-down, set-up, break-it-down system; however, we're looking at 2010 as a great year for tailgating and a great time to establish a new tradition at Aggie tailgates—the Designated Sitter.

ABOUT THE AUTHORS

Jim and Cheryl Flint '94 tailgate in Texas.

As passionate football fans, Jim and Cheryl love planning and participating in tailgating. With more than a decade's worth of active tailgating experience in College Station, the couple shares their stories and experiences in the pages of *Beyond the Tailgate*. They recently established the Jim and Cheryl Flint '94 Endowed Scholarship at Texas A&M University's College of Biomedical Sciences and Veterinary Medicine. Proceeds from sales of Beyond the Tailgate will go toward the scholarship.

OTHER BOOKS BY THE AUTHORS

Car Dog Millionaire: How to Sell Cars and Make Money at Your Internet Dealership

20/20 Vision: Actionable Insights for Digital Retailers

CITATIONS

1   http://www.tailgatingideas.com/the-top-tailgates-for-the-texas-am-tailgating-crew-part-deux/

2   http://www.tailgatingideas.com/tailgate-crashing-during-your-bye-week/

3   https://en.wikipedia.org/wiki/2006_Texas_A%26M_Aggies_football_team

4   http://www.tailgatingideas.com/the-top-12-for-the-12th-man-tailgating-crew/

5   http://www.tailgatingideas.com/the-top-12-for-the-12th-man-tailgating-crew/

6   https://en.wikipedia.org/wiki/Fundamental_attribution_error

7   http://www.tailgatingideas.com/the-top-tailgates-for-the-texas-am-tailgating-crew-part-deux/

8   http://www.tailgatingideas.com/the-top-tailgates-for-the-texas-am-tailgating-crew-part-deux/

9   http://www.tailgatingideas.com/the-top-tailgates-for-the-texas-am-tailgating-crew-part-deux/

10 https://twitter.com/Doc_Sanger

11 http://www.tailgatingideas.com/winegard-carryout-gm-1518-tailgate-approved/

12 http://www.tailgatingideas.com/cin-chili-tailgate-approved/

13 http://www.tailgatingideas.com/the-indispensible-college-football-tv-schedule-link/

14 http://www.tailgatingideas.com/the-indispensible-college-football-tv-schedule-link/

15 https://en.wikiquote.org/wiki/Inside_Out_(2015_film

16 http://www.tailgatingideas.com/texas-am-sec-tailgating-guide/

17 https://www.theeagle.com/news/local/bryan-college-station-brac-ing-for-substantial-influx-for-a-m/article_932cfc55-c7e1-586c-af03-a -646de5277e.html

18 http://www.bmbfoundation.org/

19 https://en.wikipedia.org/wiki/2018_LSU_vs._Texas_A%26M_football_game

20 http://www.tailgatingideas.com/ole-miss-chooses-academics-over-tail-gating/

21 http://www.espn.com/college-football/game?gameId=332850145

22 http://www.espn.com/college-football/story/_/id/11686868/ole-miss-vs-texas-sets-sec-attendance-record

23 https://www.usatoday.com/story/sports/ncaaf/sec/2019/02/12/ole-miss-football-vacate-33-wins-over-six-seasons-after-ncaa-probe/2845295002/

24 https://www.amazon.com/100-Year-Decision-Texas-SEC/dp/1457532328

25 https://en.wikipedia.org/wiki/Gregg_Popovich

26 http://snu.edu/trent-may-returns-to-snu-as-head-coach

27 https://www.txamfoundation.com/Spring-2017/txamfoundation.aspx

28 https://www.eventmarketer.com/article/how-brands-are-leveraging-the-tailgating-scene-to-score-with-fans/

29 https://www.amazon.com/100-Year-Decision-Texas-SEC/dp/1457532328

30 http://www.tailgatingideas.com/tailgaters-training-day/

31 https://newyork.cbslocal.com/2011/11/18/social-media-col-lides-with-traditional-tailgating/

32 https://en.wikipedia.org/wiki/Kyle_Field

33 http://www.espn.com/college-football/story/_/id/21539082/line-kev-in-sumlin-career-texas-am

34 https://www.myaggienation.com/history_traditions/12th_man/the-th-man-how-e-king-gill-started-texas-a/arti-cle_3d5df82c-0394-11e3-95ab-001a4bcf887a.html

www.ingramcontent.com/pod-product-compliance
Lightning Source LLC
Chambersburg PA
CBHW032136020426
42334CB00016B/1179